Essentials

of **Psychological Assessment** Series

Everything you need to know to administer, score, and interpret the major psychological tests.

I'd like to order the following *Essentials of Psychological Assessment:*

- ❑ WAIS®-III Assessment / 978-0-471-28295-2 • $34.95
- ❑ WJ III™ Cognitive Abilities Assessment / 978-0-471-34466-7 • $34.95
- ❑ Cross-Battery Assessment, Second Edition (w/CD-ROM) / 978-0-471-75771-9 • $44.95
- ❑ Nonverbal Assessment / 978-0-471-38318-5 • $34.95
- ❑ PAI® Assessment / 978-0-471-08463-1 • $34.95
- ❑ CAS Assessment / 978-0-471-29015-5 • $34.95
- ❑ MMPI-2™ Assessment / 978-0-471-34533-6 • $34.95
- ❑ Myers-Briggs Type Indicator® Assessment / 978-0-471-33239-8 • $34.95
- ❑ Rorschach® Assessment / 978-0-471-33146-9 • $34.95
- ❑ Millon™ Inventories Assessment, Third Edition / 978-0-470-16862-2 • $34.95
- ❑ TAT and Other Storytelling Techniques / 978-0-471-39469-3 • $34.95
- ❑ MMPI-A™ Assessment / 978-0-471-39815-8 • $34.95
- ❑ NEPSY® Assessment / 978-0-471-32690-8 • $34.95
- ❑ Neuropsychological Assessment / 978-0-471-40522-1 • $34.95
- ❑ WJ III™ Tests of Achievement Assessment / 978-0-471-33059-2 • $34.95
- ❑ Evidence-Based Academic Interventions / 978-0-470-20632-4 • $34.95
- ❑ WRAML2 and TOMAL-2 Assessment / 978-0-470-17911-6 • $34.95
- ❑ WMS®-III Assessment / 978-0-471-38080-1 • $34.95
- ❑ Behavioral Assessment / 978-0-471-35367-6 • $34.95
- ❑ Forensic Psychological Assessment / 978-0-471-33186-5 • $34.95
- ❑ Bayley Scales of Infant Development II Assessment / 978-0-471-32651-9 • $34.95
- ❑ Career Interest Assessment / 978-0-471-35365-2 • $34.95
- ❑ WPPSI™-III Assessment / 978-0-471-28895-4 • $34.95
- ❑ 16PF® Assessment / 978-0-471-23424-1 • $34.95
- ❑ Assessment Report Writing / 978-0-471-39487-7 • $34.95
- ❑ Stanford-Binet Intelligence Scales (SB5) Assessment / 978-0-471-22404-4 • $34.95
- ❑ WISC®-IV Assessment / 978-0-471-47691-7 • $34.95
- ❑ KABC-II Assessment / 978-0-471-66733-9 • $34.95
- ❑ WIAT®-II and KTEA-II Assessment / 978-0-471-70706-6 • $34.95
- ❑ Processing Assessment / 978-0-471-71925-0 • $34.95
- ❑ School Neuropsychological Assessment / 978-0-471-78372-5 • $34.95
- ❑ Cognitive Assessment with KAIT & Other Kaufman Measures / 978-0-471-38317-8 • $34.95
- ❑ Assessment with Brief Intelligence Tests / 978-0-471-26412-5 • $34.95
- ❑ Creativity Assessment / 978-0-470-13742-0 • $34.95
- ❑ WNV™ Assessment / 978-0-470-28467-4 • $34.95
- ❑ DAS-II® Assessment (w/CD-ROM) / 978-0-470-22520-2 • $44.95

Please complete the order form on the back.
To order by phone, call toll free 1-877-762-2974
To order online: www.wiley.com/essentials
To order by mail: refer to order form on next page

Essentials

of **Psychological Assessment** Series

ORDER FORM

Please send this order form with your payment (credit card or check) to:
John Wiley & Sons, Attn: J. Knott, 111 River Street, Hoboken, NJ 07030-5774

QUANTITY	TITLE	ISBN	PRICE
_____	_____	_____	_____
_____	_____	_____	_____
_____	_____	_____	_____
_____	_____	_____	_____
_____	_____	_____	_____

Shipping Charges:	Surface	2-Day	1-Day
First item	$5.00	$10.50	$17.50
Each additional item	$3.00	$3.00	$4.00
For orders greater than 15 items, please contact Customer Care at 1-877-762-2974.			

ORDER AMOUNT _____

SHIPPING CHARGES _____

SALES TAX _____

TOTAL ENCLOSED _____

NAME_____

AFFILIATION_____

ADDRESS_____

CITY/STATE/ZIP _____

TELEPHONE _____

EMAIL_____

❑ Please add me to your e-mailing list

PAYMENT METHOD:

❑ Check/Money Order   ❑ Visa   ❑ Mastercard   ❑ AmEx

Card Number _____ Exp. Date _____

Cardholder Name (Please print) _____

Signature _____

*Make checks payable to **John Wiley & Sons.** Credit card orders invalid if not signed.*
All orders subject to credit approval. • Prices subject to change.

To order by phone, call toll free 1-877-762-2974
To order online: www.wiley.com/essentials

Essentials of
Creativity Assessment

Essentials of Psychological Assessment Series
Series Editors, Alan S. Kaufman and Nadeen L. Kaufman

Essentials

of Creativity

Assessment

James C. Kaufman

Jonathan A. Plucker

John Baer

John Wiley & Sons, Inc.

WILEY

Library of Congress Cataloging-in-Publication Data:

Kaufman, James C.
    Essentials of creativity assessment / by James C. Kaufman, Jonathan A. Plucker, John Baer.
       p. cm.
    Includes bibliographical references and index.
    ISBN 978-0-470-13742-0 (pbk.)
    1. Creative ability—Testing. I. Plucker, Jonathan A., 1969– II. Baer, John. III. Title.
BF433.07K38 2008
153.3'50287—dc22

                                                                          2008008343

Printed in the United States of America

10 9 8 7 6 5 4 3 2 1

To my best friend since high school, my best man,
and like me, a baseball fan despite it all:
Nate Stone.—JK

To my wife, Kathleen, for all of her support,
understanding, and friendship.—JP

For Sylvia—JB

CONTENTS

ACKNOWLEDGMENTS

We would like to thank:

- Isabel Pratt, Lisa Gebo, Sweta Gupta, and everyone at Wiley who has been so helpful on this project
- Series Editors Alan and Nadeen Kaufman, for their support
- Stacy Brooks, Matthew Makel, and Kristina Rosenau for editorial assistance, and Sarah Burgess for extensive help with preparing the manuscript
- Our colleagues Ronald Beghetto, Christine Charyton, Zorana Ivcevic, Paul Silvia, Robert Sternberg, and Xiangdong Yang for their input and suggestions

SERIES PREFACE

In the *Essentials of Psychological Assessment* series, we have attempted to provide the reader with books that will deliver key practical information in the most efficient and accessible style. The series features instruments in a variety of domains, such as cognition, personality, education, and neuropsychology. For the experienced clinician, books in the series will offer a concise yet thorough way to master utilization of the continuously evolving supply of new and revised instruments, as well as a convenient method for keeping up to date on the tried-and-true measures. The novice will find here a prioritized assembly of all the information and techniques that must be at one's fingertips to begin the complicated process of individual psychological diagnosis.

Wherever feasible, visual shortcuts to highlight key points are utilized alongside systematic, step-by-step guidelines. Chapters are focused and succinct. Topics are targeted for an easy understanding of the essentials of administration, scoring, interpretation, and clinical application. Theory and research are continually woven into the fabric of each book, but always to enhance clinical inference, never to sidetrack or overwhelm. We have long been advocates of what has been called *intelligent testing*—the notion that a profile of test scores is meaningless unless it is brought to life by the clinical observations and astute detective work of knowledgeable examiners. Test profiles must be used to make a difference in the child's or adult's life, or why bother to test? We want this series to help our readers become the best intelligent testers they can be.

In *Essentials of Creativity Assessment*, Drs. James C. Kaufman, Jonathan A. Plucker, and John Baer cover the wide field of creativity assessment. These three international leaders in the field outline the major ideas in creativity research and both discuss and evaluate common creativity measures such as divergent thinking tests, the consensual technique, peer/teacher assessment, and self-assessment. They link creativity, intelligence, and giftedness in an insightful manner, and they present a list of take-home points to remember on the diverse topics covered in this cutting-edge book.

Alan S. Kaufman, PhD, and Nadeen L. Kaufman, EdD, Series Editors
Yale University School of Medicine

Essentials of
Creativity Assessment

One

INTRODUCTION TO CREATIVITY

What does it mean to be creative? Some might say thinking outside the box; others might argue it's having a good imagination, and still others might suggest creativity is a synergy that can be tapped through brainstorming. We take an empirical, psychological approach to this question. One of the first things we want to do is to define what we believe creativity is.

We are starting off with a definition for creativity because so many studies on creativity do *not* define the construct. Plucker, Beghetto, and Dow (2004) selected 90 different articles that either appeared in the two top creativity journals or articles in a different peer-reviewed journal with the word "creativity" in the title. Of these papers, only 38 percent explicitly defined what creativity was. For the purpose of this book, we will use the definition proposed by Plucker et al. (2004):

"Creativity is the interaction among aptitude, process, and environment by which an individual or group produces a perceptible product that is both novel and useful as defined within a social context" (p. 90).

Through this book, we may refer to a creative person, the creative process, a creative environment, or a creative product. We will discuss in this book how a product is determined to be new and/or useful and appropriate, who are the best judges, and what ratings may stand the test of time. We will also discuss ways of identifying creative people, either for guidance or admission to a program or school.

> **DON'T FORGET**
> ....
> Creativity is the interaction among aptitude, process, and environment by which an individual or group produces a perceptible product that is both novel and useful as defined within a social context.

As we will discuss, creativity is a key component of human cognition that is related yet distinct from the construct of intelligence. A school psychologist who is presenting a complete perspective on an individual's abilities may wish to include creativity as part of this assessment. However, it is often difficult to find or to decipher creativity assessments. They may seem like "pop" psychology, they may lack the standard psychometric information that is present in IQ tests, and they may require resources that a typical school psychologist may not possess (for example, access to five expert poets). We are writing this book to gather all as many resources as possible together so that you can make your own judgment about the best creativity assessments. There is no one perfect test for creativity, and we won't even always agree on the best possible measures. But we believe that after reading this book, you will be able to select a method for assessing creativity that best fits whatever situations, groups of people, and programs you may encounter.

A BRIEF OVERVIEW OF THE STUDY OF CREATIVITY

One way of organizing creativity research is the "Four P" model, which distinguishes the creative person, process, product, and press (i.e., environment) (Rhodes, 1961). We will use this model as a way of briefly highlighting theories and research that will be helpful background material in reading this book. We want to emphasize that this overview is just a highlight; there are numerous books devoted to the study of creativity. For recent books that give more detailed information about these ideas, we would recommend Piirto (2004), Runco (2006), Sawyer (2006), Simonton (2004), Sternberg (2003), and Weisberg (2006), as well as edited volumes such as Dorfman, Locher, and Martindale (2006), Kaufman and Baer (2005, 2006), Kaufman and Sternberg (2006), Sternberg (1999a), and Sternberg, Grigorenko, and Singer (2004). We emphasize that we have only mentioned a handful out of many possible books, with a focus on recent works.

The Creative Person

Studies of the creative person may look at individual characteristics of the creator. These areas may include personality, motivation, intelligence, thinking styles, emotional intelligence, or knowledge (e.g., Baer & Kaufman, 2005; Sternberg & Lubart, 1995). Sternberg and Lubart (1995), in their Investment Theory, proposed that creative thinkers are like good investors—they buy low and sell high, or invest time and energy in currently unpopular ideas that have great potential for solving different types of problems. Investors do so in the world of finance, whereas creative people use ideas as currency.

Another theory that focuses on the creative person (and, as we will see later, also deals with creative environments) is Amabile's (1983, 1996) componential model of creativity. This theory proposed that three variables were needed for creativity to occur: domain-relevant skills, creativity-relevant skills, and task motivation. Domain-relevant skills include knowledge, technical skills, and specialized talents that individuals might possess that are important in particular domains, but not in others. If you're going to be a creative doctor, according to this theory, you would need to know medicine, but that medical knowledge might be of little use to someone who wanted to be a creative composer of music. Creativity-relevant skills are personal factors that are associated with creativity more generally, across many or all domains, such as tolerance for ambiguity, self-discipline, and a willingness to take appropriate risks. If one focuses on the individual person as possessor of such skills, the emphasis is on the person, but if one's focus is on the underlying cognitive skill, then the emphasis is on the process itself rather than the person possessing it.

The third component in Amabile's model singles out one's motivation toward the task at hand. Intrinsic motivation—being driven by enjoyment of a task—is more associated with creativity than extrinsic motivation, or being driven by external rewards such as money or praise. A preference or need for a particular kind of motivation can be either domain-specific or domain-general. Someone might find learning and thinking about many different kinds of ideas very intrinsically motivating and need no outside reward to undertake such wide-ranging studies, or, on the other hand, someone might lack intrinsic motivation to do these things and might need extrinsic rewards to do any such studying. Either way, this would represent a very general intrinsic or extrinsic orientation toward motivation. But it is also common for someone to have a great deal of intrinsic motivation when it comes to some things, such as writing poetry, but it might require a great deal of extrinsic motivation in the form of rewards or anticipated evaluation to get that same person to think about doing something like a science project. It is also true that sometimes motivation can be thought of as something an individual possesses, whereas other times it's more the other way around: the environment (press) "possesses" the person, making either intrinsic or extrinsic motivation much more salient, at least temporarily.

Many of the methods described in the chapters of this book focus on the assessment

> ## DON'T FORGET
> ....
> Intrinsic motivation—doing something because it is interesting or inherently rewarding to do—is more associated with creativity than extrinsic motivation—doing something either to earn an external reward (such as money or praise) or because one is concerned about how one's work will be evaluated. A preference for a particular kind of motivation can be either domain-specific or domain-general.

of the creativity of individuals. For example, there are various methods of self-assessment and assessment by others that emphasize how creative a person is, either generally or in particular domains. (See Rapid Reference 1.1.)

≡ *Rapid Reference 1.1*

The Four P's of Creativity

Person

Process

Press (Environment)

Product

The Creative Process

The creative process is the actual experience of being creative. One popular conception is the idea of flow, or optimal experience, which refers to the sensations and feelings that come when an individual is intensely engaged in an activity (Csikszentmihalyi, 1996). One could experience flow in anything from rock climbing to playing the piano. An individual must feel like his or her abilities are a match for the potential challenges of the situation to enter the flow state. Early work on flow asked participants to wear electronic paging devices. The study participants were then beeped at random times (during the day, not at three in the morning) and asked to fill out forms that asked what they were doing and how they were feeling (Graef, Csikszentmihalyi, & Giannino, 1983; Larson & Csikszentmihalyi, 1983; Prescott, Csikszentmihalyi, & Graef, 1981). Later work revolved around interviews with acclaimed people, many known for being creative (Csikszentmihalyi, 1996; Perry, 1999).

Another way of considering the creative process is found in

DON'T FORGET

Flow is the experience of being intensely engaged in an activity. Someone could experience flow from a creative activity, such as playing the guitar or writing a computer program, or from a physical activity, such as rock climbing.

the Geneplore Model (Finke, Ward, & Smith, 1996). This framework has two phases—generative and exploratory. Generation, the "novel" part, is generating many different ideas in which a mental representation is formed of a possible creative solution. In the generative phase someone constructs a preinventive structure, or a mental representation of a possible creative solution. Exploration refers to evaluating these possible options and choosing the best one (or ones). There may be several cycles before a creative work is produced.

Many assessments focus on creativity-relevant skills or processes, such as the Torrance Tests of Creative Thinking and other measures of divergent thinking. The ability to find similarities among seemingly disparate words, as measured by the Remote Associates Test, is another example of a creativity assessment technique that focuses on processes. As with assessments of persons, assessments of skills or processes can look at creativity-relevant thinking skills more generally, or they can instead focus on skills that may be important only in particular domains. The most widely used divergent-thinking tests, for example, are the Torrance Tests of Creative Thinking, which assess divergent-thinking skill generally via two different versions, one verbal and the other figural.

The Creative Press

The third "P," press, can refer to either home or work environment. Amabile (1996) has done many studies that consider the importance for creativity of intrinsic motivation, or being driven by a passion for the activity. People who enjoy the job at hand will generally also be more creative. Amabile and Gryskiewicz (1989) identify eight aspects of the work environment that stimulate creativity: adequate freedom, challenging work, appropriate resources, a supportive supervisor, diverse and communicative coworkers, recognition, a sense of cooperation, and an organization that supports creativity. They also list four aspects that restrain creativity: time pressure, too much evaluation, an emphasis on keeping the status quo, and too much organizational politics. Studies of the creative press (or environment) are often designed to determine how the context in which one works or studies may be modified to encourage people to be more creative.

Environment doesn't have to mean a work environment; other research has examined home background and childhood and how these early experiences are related to creativity. Sulloway (1996) found that the first-born child was more likely to achieve power and privilege, but later-born children were more likely to be open to experience and revolutionary. This trend extends across many domains; if you examine how prominent scientists reacted when Darwin proposed his classic (and controversial) theory of natural selection, 83 percent of the people who supported the theory were later-born children, and only 17 percent were first-born (Sulloway, 1996). This birth-order effect, although statistically significant, is actually rather small, as is the parallel effect in the area of intelligence (first-borns tend to have slightly higher IQs than later-born children). These are interesting findings (and ones that have generated lots of publicity for such studies, which unlike most psychological studies are frequently reported in the popular press), but the sizes of these effects are generally so small that they are of no practical use as methods of assessing either the creativity or intelligence of individuals.

Other kinds of life events can also influence later creative productivity. Simonton (1994) reviews many studies that both demonstrate and empirically show, for example, that losing a parent before age 10 is much more common in eminent people (as opposed to non-eminent). Other disasters that are more likely to befall the well known include bouts of poverty, physical illness, and mental illness (e.g., Ludwig, 1995). How-

CAUTION

Although first-borns and latter-borns differ on some traits relevant to creativity, the differences, while statistically significant, are so small that they are of no practical use in assessing either creativity or intelligence.

ever, it is important to note that such findings should be considered carefully; it is easy for such stories of childhood trauma to be inflated for dramatic purposes (such as in a biography).

One theory that focuses on the relationship of a creator to the environment is the Systems Model proposed by Csikszentmihalyi (1996). This model considers creativity to be a byproduct of the domain (i.e., mathematics), the field (the gatekeepers, such as editors and critics), and the person. In this model, these three elements work interactively.

Creativity assessment does not often focus on the environment when assessing individuals. Evaluations of the creativity-inducing or creativity-inhibiting aspects of environments can be very important in designing school and working settings, but rarely are such environmental evaluations part of the assessment of individual creativity, except perhaps retrospectively in the biographies of famous creators.

The Creative Product

The creative product—the things people make, the ideas they express, the responses they give—will be the focus of much of this book; most creativity assessments (not all) tend to focus on a tangible product (such as a poem, a drawing, or responses to an open-ended question or problem).

In some cases, as in the method called the Consensual Assessment Technique (CAT), the focus is exclusively on the product itself. Expert judges assign creativity ratings to actual products (such as a poem or a collage). These experts tend to agree with each other on what is creative (which is why the term "consensual" is appropriate). In other cases, such as the tests of divergent thinking mentioned earlier, the product (the responses to an open-ended question that a test-taker gives) are the raw material used to infer the thinking processes and skills used by that person. One difference between product-focused assessments, such as the CAT, and process-focused assessments, such as the TTCT, is that products are typically domain-specific; in other words, a product might be a poem, a musical composition, or a mathematical proof. The question of domain specificity versus domain generality is one of the major unresolved issues in creativity research (Are the traits, knowledge, skills, habits, or whatever else leads to creativity things that influence creativity in *all* areas, or only in limited areas?). In fact, two of this book's authors took opposing views on this issue in the only point-counterpoint pair of articles ever published in the *Creativity Research Journal* (Baer, 1998; Plucker, 1998). As with many such disputes, the truth may lie somewhere in between, as in the hierarchical APT Model of creativity, which posits both general factors that impact creativity in all areas and several levels of domain-specific factors that impact creative performance in increasingly narrow ranges of activities (Baer & Kaufman, 2005; Kaufman & Baer, 2004, 2005).

One theory of creative products is the Propulsion Model (Sternberg, Kaufman, & Pretz, 2005), which outlines eight types of possible creative contributions based on their relationship to a field. The first four contributions all stay within the framework of an existing paradigm; one example is forward incrementation, in which a product moves the field forward in a direction just a little bit (such as a modification to an existing scientific theory). The final four types of creative contributions represent attempts to reject and replace the current paradigm. One example is reinitiation, in which the creator tries to move the field to a new (as-yet-unreached) starting point and then progress from there; an example might be James Joyce's *Ulysses*. (See Rapid Reference 1.2.)

Some assessment techniques focus on one particular part of the creativity puzzle—the

≡ *Rapid Reference 1.2*

Propulsion Model

The propulsion model of creativity considers the impact of a creative contribution to its field. This model is typically used for eminent creativity.

person, the process, the product, or the press, as noted above. Other methods consider more than one aspect of creativity, as also noted. Some approaches to assessing creativity are also clearly under-written by particular theories of creativity, such as the divergent-production model that underlies all divergent-thinking tests. Other approaches, such as the Consensual Assessment Technique, are not tied to particular theoretical models of how creativity works. In the chapters that follow, we will point out particular theoretical commitments of some of the assessment techniques we describe when such connections are important.

ADDING CREATIVITY AS AN ASSESSMENT TOOL

We believe that creativity is a natural candidate to supplement traditional measures of ability and achievement. A growing trend among admission committees and educators is a focus on non-cognitive constructs, such as emotional intelligence, motivation, and creativity, to supplement current measures (Kyllonen, Walters, & Kaufman, 2002). Creativity is a prime candidate to be such a supplement. One reason (as we will discuss in Chapter Six) is that creativity is related to intelligence and academic ability, yet not so closely related as to not account for additional variance. Another promising reason is the reduction in gender and ethnicity differences. Finally, many facets of education have highlighted a specific interest in the measurement of creativity.

Reform efforts in school standards, for example, are showing a renewed interest in literature and creative writing (*Standards for the English/Language Arts,* 1996). More than 50 colleges have decided to offer creative writing majors in recent years (bringing the total to more than 300); this increase comes at a time when the number of English majors as a whole is decreasing (Bartlett, 2002). A survey of distinguished graduate faculty members found that creativity was considered to be one of the most important competencies deemed essential for success in graduate school (Enright & Gitomer, 1989). Creativity was one of six non-cognitive areas that Mayer (2001) recommended as being valuable candidates for new measures, and creativity was one of five qualities singled out in a study of potential additional measures to the GRE (Walpole, Burton, Kanyi, & Jackenthal, 2001).

The fact that creativity is not assessed on current measures of ability and achievement is often cited by testing opponents as one reason why these tests are not valid or significant. Paul Houston, executive director of the American Association of School Administrators, has said, "Children today need critical thinking skills, creativity, perseverance, and integrity—qualities not measured on a standardized test" (Assessment Reform Network, 2002). In a similar vein, former U.S. Secretary of Labor Robert Reich wrote, "Many new jobs depend on creativity—on out-of-the-box thinking, originality, and flair . . . Standardized tests can't measure these sorts of things" (Reich, 2001). Whether standardized tests can or cannot measure creativity, it is possible to measure creativity on an individual basis—and this measurement can supplement traditional measures and increase fairness in assessment.

The next chapter will focus on divergent thinking assessment, perhaps the most common form of creativity measurement. Chapter three will cover the Consensual Assessment Technique in greater detail. Chapters four and five will cover assessments by others (teachers, peers, parents) and self, respectively. Chapter six will discuss the relationship between creativity and intelligence, and chapter seven will take a look forward.

🖋 TEST YOURSELF 🖋

1. **Which of the following is NOT part of the "Four P" model?**

   (a) Process

   (b) Product

   (c) Possibility

   (d) Person

2. **Which of the following is most commonly associated with creativity?**

   (a) Intrinsic motivation

   (b) Extrinsic motivation

   (c) Anticipation of rewards

   (d) Anticipation of evaluation

3. **The two phases of the Geneplore Model are:**

   (a) buying low and selling high

   (b) intelligence and achievement

   (c) generation and exploration

   (d) intrinsic and extrinsic motivation

4. **The Torrance Tests of Creative Thinking assess:**

   (a) task motivation

   (b) domain-specific knowledge

   (c) artistic ability

   (d) divergent thinking

5. **Levels of intrinsic motivation tend to:**

   (a) be independent of the environments in which one works

   (b) vary within the same individual across different domains

   (c) be consistent within the same individual across different domains

   (d) influence intelligence more than creativity

6. "Flow" refers to:

(a) the speed at which one works

(b) consistency among items in a divergent-thinking test

(c) similarities between intelligence and creativity test scores

(d) the experience of being intensely engaged in an activity

Answers: 1. c; 2. a; 3. c; 4. d; 5. b; 6. d

Two

DIVERGENT THINKING TESTS

One of the great ironies of the study of creativity is that so much energy and effort have been focused on a single class of assessments: measures of divergent thinking. In other words, there's not much divergence in the history of creativity assessment. We'll talk about why this is not necessarily a bad thing later in the chapter, and there is certainly much more work to do in this area, but it is impossible to consider creativity assessments without examination of the voluminous research on divergent thinking tasks.

One housekeeping note before we start: The nomenclature surrounding the use of these assessments is diverse. Over the past several decades, authors have referred to them as tests, tasks, and assessments, among other labels (Wallach and Kogan probably wouldn't object to the term "games" or "activities"). In this book, we will primarily refer to them as divergent thinking tests or divergent thinking tasks, although the reader should be forgiving if we use other terms. We will also refer to divergent thinking as DT at various points to streamline the discussion.

Back to the action. Divergent thinking is clearly the backbone of creativity assessment and has held this key position for many decades.[1]

---

1. So much so, in fact, that we cannot possibly cover the topic comprehensively in one chapter and instead focus on the main themes related to DT assessment. We strongly encourage interested readers to read the major reviews of the topic, including Guilford (1967b) and Runco (1991, 1992a, 1999).

Articles on divergent thinking frequently appear in the major creativity journals, most books on creativity include lengthy discussions of divergent thinking (some focus on it nearly exclusively), school districts frequently use DT tests to identify creative potential, and DT tests are used extensively around the world to assess creativity. We have personally witnessed high-priced business consultants conducting "creativity training sessions" for Fortune 500 companies that consist almost exclusively of repackaged DT activities and assessments from the early 1970s.[2] DT may not be the only game in Creativity Town, but its continued importance cannot be disputed.

This status is probably due to several interrelated factors. First, the majority of creativity assessment work from the 1950s through the 1970s—and even into the 1980s—focused on divergent thinking. Indeed, given the perceived overemphasis on convergent skills at the time, the push to emphasize divergent aspects of cognition was understandable. As Guilford (1968) noted, "Most of our problem solving in everyday life involves divergent thinking. Yet in our educational practices, we tend to emphasize teaching students how to find conventional answers" (p. 8).[3] As creativity became popular in the 1960s (and was supported by considerable federal funding in the United States), much of the research and practical application dealt with divergent thinking and related assessments. This work serves as the foundation for all current efforts to understand creativity, hence the continued emphasis on DT in many current scholars' work.

Second, many of the major figures in creativity research and education have been fascinated with the role of divergent thinking in creativity. J. P. Guilford, Paul Torrance, Michael Wallach, Nathan Kogan,

---

2. For a healthy five figure fee per day. Seriously.

3. Ironically, and somewhat depressingly, the past 10-15 years has seen a national level re-emphasis on convergent thinking, so Guilford's observation is still relevant today – perhaps more than ever before.

DON'T FORGET

Many of the top creativity researchers have studied divergent thinking.

Joseph Renzulli, and Mark Runco, among many others, conducted (or are conducting) major lines of inquiry involving DT. Given that many of these scholars are also major figures in the social sciences in general, the continued influence of their DT work on the field of creative studies is not surprising.

Third, developments in the assessment of intelligence in the 20th Century probably put significant pressure on creativity researchers to follow a parallel path in the measurement of creativity. Psychometrics were a powerful force in the previous century, and as creativity became a hot topic in mid-century it was natural for researchers to look to other major areas of psychological assessment for inspiration, with intelligence foremost among these areas. Given the rather undifferentiated conceptions of creativity that existed in those years, pushing hard to develop DT tests was perfectly logical. In essence, intelligence test envy was a powerful force. That's a bit strong, but probably pretty accurate.

Fourth, and perhaps most important, there is a legitimate case to be made that divergent thinking is a key component of creativity and, more specifically, creative problem solving. Divergent thinking can be conceptualized as involving cognitive processes that help one produce multiple responses to open-ended questions or problems. DT is often contrasted with convergent thinking, in which cognitive processes are used to produce one or very few possible solutions to a given problem.

Historically, divergent and convergent thinking have been treated as distinct sets of processes, although Runco (2007) and Eysenck (2003), among others, have proposed that they lie on a continuum of cognitive processes. Runco (2007) helpfully extends this argument by noting that it is more useful to utilize the continuum perspective because very few problems (if any) in the real world require only divergent or convergent thinking.

WHAT IS DIVERGENT THINKING?

The usefulness of divergent thinking is obvious, hence its importance within the study of creativity and problem solving. As the British Prime Minister Benjamin Disraeli once noted about a political opponent, "He had only one idea, and it was wrong." When problem solving, the divergent thinker simply has a fuller cognitive toolbox from which to pull potential solutions, which from a statistical perspective suggests a greater chance of solving a problem than someone with fewer, less original ideas.

Runco (1999) has provided perhaps the clearest, most succinct definition: "Divergent thinking is cognition that leads in various directions" (p. 577). In defining divergent thinking, Guilford (1968) makes a clear distinction with convergent thinking:

> In convergent-thinking tests, the examinee must arrive at one right answer. The information given generally is sufficiently structured so that there is only one right answer. . . . [A]n example with verbal material would be: "What is *the* opposite of hard?" In divergent thinking, the thinker must do much searching around, and often a number of answers will do or are wanted. If you ask the examinee to name all the things he can think of that are hard, also edible, also white, he has a whole class of things that might do. It is in the divergent-thinking category that we find the abilities that are most significant in creative thinking and invention. (p. 8, emphasis in original)

Torrance (1970) struck a similar chord when he placed the teaching of divergent thinking firmly within his conceptualization of creative teaching:

> Learning by authority appears primarily to involve such abilities as recognition, memory, and logical reasoning, which are, incidentally, the abilities most frequently assessed by traditional intelligence tests and measures of scholastic aptitude. In contrast, learning creatively through creative and problem-solving

DON'T FORGET

....

The four key aspects of divergent thinking are fluency, originality, flexibility, and elaboration.

activities, in addition to recognition, memory, and logical reasoning, requires . . . evaluation . . . , divergent production . . . , and redefinition. (p. 2)

Four aspects of divergent thinking that are frequently mentioned in the literature are:

Fluency   The number of responses to a given stimuli, "the total number of ideas given on any one divergent thinking exercise" (Runco, 1999, p. 577)

Originality The uniqueness of responses to a given stimuli, "the unusualness . . . of an examinee's or respondent's ideas" (Runco, 1999, p. 577)

Flexibility   The number and/or uniqueness of categories of responses to a given stimuli, or more broadly, "a change in the meaning, use, or interpretation of something." (Guilford, 1968, p. 99)

Elaboration The extension of ideas within a specific category of responses to a given stimuli, "to fill [ideas] out with details." (Guilford, 1967, p. 138)

For example, if a person were planning a social occasion at a restaurant to celebrate a special occasion, she may want to produce a list of possible locations. She may produce a list of 50 potential restaurants (high fluency), a list that includes restaurants her friends would be unlikely to think about (high originality), a list with a wide range of types of restaurants (high flexibility), or a list that includes only Indian restaurants but lists every possible such establishment in the area (high elaboration). At some point, she will need to propose one or two restaurants to the group, which will require evaluative and convergent processes.

The four aspects can be broken down further. For example, Guilford (1967) found support in the literature for four kinds of fluency (word, ideational, associational, and expressional), two kinds of flexibility (spontaneous, adaptive), and a differentiated concept of originality. Interestingly, although these distinctions are well supported in the research literature, many contemporary approaches to DT focus on the traditional aspects of fluency, originality, flexibility, and elaboration.

A VERY BRIEF HISTORY OF DIVERGENT THINKING AND ITS ASSESSMENT

Divergent thinking is best understood as emerging from earlier traditions of the study of creativity. The origins of these traditions are difficult to trace, but Rhodes (1961) is often credited with categorizing approaches to creativity as focusing on the *person,* the *process* of creating, the creative *product,* and the *environment* in which creativity occurs. With a little creativity—replacing *environment* with *place* or *press*—this categorization has become knows as the Four P's of Creativity and remains widely used today.[4]

In contrast to today's predominant systems theories, which also consider varied perspectives and influences on the development of creativity, the Four P approach generally studied each of the four aspects in isolation (not uncommon in the social sciences at that point in history). The creative person, exemplified by the work of Frank Barron and Donald MacKinnon at the Institute for Personality Assessment and Research (see Barron, 1988), and creative process, in the form of divergent thinking, received the lion's share of academic attention during this period (see Guilford, 1967, Chapter 6, for an overview of early

---

4. Taylor (1988) credited Mooney (1963) for creating the Four P's.

work on divergent thinking, and Torrance, 1979, for a discussion of the focus on person and process approaches).

The cornerstone of these divergent thinking efforts was the use of various tests of divergent thinking. Divergent thinking tests require individuals to produce several responses to a specific prompt, in sharp contrast to most standardized tests of achievement or ability that require one correct answer. This emphasis on fluency, also referred to as ideational fluency or simply ideation, is seen as a key component of creative processes, although it is clearly not the only component.

Although the development of measures of DT is generally seen as a mid-20th century development, divergent thinking was of interest to psychologists and educators for several years earlier. For example, Runco (2007) notes that Alfred Binet and his colleagues included divergent thinking items on their tests of intelligence, and Torrance (1988) discussed the earlier thoughts of L. L. Thurstone about originality and its evaluation.

However, Guilford's development of DT tests in the 1950s and 1960s is usually considered to be the launching point for serious development efforts and large-scale application. Among the first measures of divergent thinking were Guilford's (1967b) Structure of the Intellect (SOI) divergent production tests, Wallach and Kogan's (1965) and Getzels and Jackson's (1962) divergent thinking tests, and Torrance's (1962, 1974) Tests of Creative Thinking (TTCT).

MAJOR APPROACHES TO DT ASSESSMENT

The SOI Assessments

Extending far beyond the various types of divergent thinking that he had identified in the literature, Guilford's (1967b) Structure of the Intellect Model proposed 24 distinct types of divergent thinking: One type for each combination of four types of content (Figural, Symbolic,

Semantic, Behavioral) and six types of product (Units, Classes, Relations, Systems, Transformations, Implications).[5] For example, the SOI DT battery consists of several tests on which subjects are asked to exhibit evidence of divergent production in several areas, including divergent production of semantic units (e.g., listing consequences of people no longer needing to sleep), of figural classes (finding as many classifications of sets of figures as is possible), and of figural units (taking a simple shape such as a circle and elaborating upon it as often as possible).

Another example is the Match Problem, which represented the divergent production of figural transformations. The Match Problem has several variations, but they tend to be variations on the basic theme of Match Problem I. In this test, 17 matches are placed to create a grid of two rows and three columns (i.e., six squares). Participants are asked to remove three matches so that the remaining matches form four complete squares. Guilford (1967b) noted that such tasks are characterized by the need for trial-and-error strategies and flexible thinking (i.e., "desert[ing] what was probably a common assumption, e.g., that the remaining squares . . . should all be of the same size," p. 152). Several other tests were also used to study figural transformations, all with the same basic requirements to come up with multiple ways to transform visual-spatial objects and relationships. Guilford believed that this particular group of tests assesses flexibility.

Guilford's entire SOI divergent production battery consists of several dozen such tests corresponding to the various divergent thinking components, and representative tests from the battery are presented in Table 2.1. Meeker and colleagues (1969; Meeker & Meeker, 1982;

---

5. Guilford made several changes to the SOI models that generally increased the number of cells. For example, in 1988 he published a revision that split the figural content into auditory and visual content. For our purposes, the number of DT-related SOI is immaterial other than noting that the number is large.

Table 2.1. Examples of Guilford DT Tests

Dimension	Test	Example
Figural Units	Sketches	Drawing as many objects as possible using a basic figure, such as a circle [fluency]
Symbolic Units	Suffixes	Listing as many words as possible given a specific suffix [fluency]
Semantic Units	Consequences (obvious)	Listing commonly mentioned consequences of a impossible event, such as people not needing to sleep [fluency]
Semantic Units	Utility	List uses for a common object (e.g., brick, pencil) [fluency]
Figural Classes	Alternate Letter Groups	Given a set of letters, forming subgroups according to the figural aspects of the letters [flexibility]
Symbolic Classes	Name Grouping	Given a set of names, forming subgroups based on different rules (e.g., number of syllables, starts with a vowel) [flexibility]
Semantic Relations	Controlled Associations	Given eight words, listing words with similar meanings [fluency]
Figural Systems	Making Objects	Given four shapes, using at least two of them to make a new object [fluency]
Semantic Transformations	Consequences (remote)	Using the same prompt as Consequences (obvious), but scoring only those responses that are unique [originality]
Semantic Transformations	Associations I	Given two words, finding a third word that links the two (e.g., movie and fishing are linked by reel) [originality]
Semantic Transformations	Alternate Signs	Drawing up to six symbols to represent a given concept [originality]
Figural Implications	Figure Production	Adding lines to a simple figure (e.g., two lines) to create a new figure [elaboration]

Note. Drawn from Guilford (1967b) and the research cited therein.

Meeker, Meeker, & Roid, 1985) developed a version of the SOI tests, the Structure of the Intellect-Learning Abilities Test (SOI-LA), to diagnose weaknesses in divergent thinking (among other areas) that can then be addressed by remediation. The SOI-LA consists of 26 subtests, with each subtest corresponding to one dimension of the SOI model. The SOI-LA includes DT subtests for divergent production of Figural Units, Symbolic Relations, and Semantic Units.

Guilford and his colleagues gathered enormous amounts of assessment data in order to validate the SOI model. The archives still exist and have frequently been accessed in order to analyze the data with advanced statistical methods. In addition, other large databases have been used to examine the validity evidence. The results of these analyses are generally supportive of the SOI model (e.g., Chen Shyuefee & Michael, 1993; Guilford & Hoepfner, 1966; Holly & Michael, 1972), although occasionally researchers have suggested revisions to the model (Chen Shyuefee & Michael, 1993; Michael & Bachelor, 1992) or concluded that the model has serious weaknesses (Alliger, 1988; Sternberg & Grigorenko, 2000–2001). Psychometric evaluations of the SOI-LA have also generally been favorable regarding reliability and concurrent validity estimates (Cunningham, Thompson, Ashton, & Wakefield, 1978; Meeker et al., 1985), although the psychometric integrity of the test is not without its critics (e.g., Clarizio & Mehrens, 1985; Coffman, 1985; Cummings, 1989).

"Guilford-like" Tests

A number of researchers in the early 1960s published results of studies that relied heavily on SOI-like assessments, including Raymond Cattell for parts of his Objective-Analytic Test Battery (see Cattell & Butcher, 1968, Chap. 14). For example, the Instances Test requires that students list as many things that move on wheels (things that make noise, etc.) as possible (Wallach & Kogan, 1965; Wallach & Wing, 1969), and on variations of the Uses Test students provide responses to prompts such as "Tell me all the different ways you could use a chair" (newspaper, knife, tire) (Wallach & Kogan, 1965, p. 31) or bricks, pencils, and toothpicks (Getzels & Jackson, 1962). Wallach and Wing (1969) describe the pattern-meanings task as a series of abstract forms that "simply served to provide representationally ambiguous visual materials that would be open to numerous alternative interpretations" with the instructions to "write down all the different things you can think of that each complete pattern might suggest." Other tests included word association, embedded figures, story completion, problem construction, and line interpretation problems (Getzels & Jackson, 1962; Wallach & Kogan, 1965). These tests were all scored for fluency and originality, with high inter-rater agreement.

The most appreciable difference between the various batteries developed in this period lies in the conditions in which students take the tests. Wallach and Kogan (1965) supported game-like, untimed administration of divergent thinking tasks, which they believed allows creativity to be measured distinctly from intelligence due to the creation of "a frame of reference which is relatively free from the coercion of time limits and relatively free from the stress of knowing that one's behavior is under close evaluation" (p. 24). This constraint-free administration is in contrast to the test-like, timed procedures used with most other divergent thinking measures and addresses the concerns of several scholars who, like Torrance (1970), worried that "Children are so accustomed to the one correct or best answer that they may be reluctant to think of other possibilities or to build up a pool of ideas to be evaluated later" (p. 86).

These studies essentially sought to establish a link between psychometric approaches of intelligence and creativity, with Getzels and Jackson finding almost complete overlap and Wallach and Kogan finding evidence of largely distinct constructs (which they attributed to their administration of DT tests in non-test-like conditions).

Wallach and Wing, in their study of incoming college freshmen, also found little overlap between intelligence (SAT scores) and ideation (number and uniqueness of ideas). Interestingly, they concluded that ideation was the more important predictor of achievement outside of the classroom, which they believed to be a better predictor of life success, and recommended that college admissions policies adapt accordingly.

These tests, especially the prompts asking for similarities, alternate uses, and instances, remain popular, especially in the research literature (e.g., Chan et al., 2000–2001; Charles & Runco, 2000–2001; Plucker, Runco, & Lim, 2006).

The Torrance Tests of Creative Thinking

The Torrance Tests of Creative Thinking (TTCT; Torrance, 1966, 1968, 1972, 1974, 1984, 1988, 1990, 2008), which are also based upon many aspects of the SOI battery, are by far the most commonly used tests of divergent thinking and continue to enjoy widespread international use (e.g., Aslan & Puccio, 2006; Niu, 2007; Wechsler, 2006). In a review of published creativity research, Torrance and Presbury (1984) found that the TTCT were used in the majority of research studies on creativity up to that point in the field's history. Roughly a decade later, Callahan et al. (1995) found the Torrance Tests to be a popular measure for identifying creative potential for gifted education programs.

Torrance (1968) wrote that these tests "represent a fairly sharp departure from the factor type tests developed by Guilford and his associates" (p. 167), and he continued in the same article to differentiate his work from that of Wallach and Kogan (although he noted a desire to "retain in the test instructions and format some of the invitation to play or regress cultivated by Wallach and Kogan," p. 167). This "sharp departure" is more evident in the early versions of Torrance's work, and many of the tasks on the most recent forms of the TTCT are very similar to those of Guilford and related tests (not surprisingly, given the dozens of tasks Guilford used to assess DT; i.e., there are only so many truly unique ways to assess verbal and figural fluency).[6]

This is not to say that Torrance's work was not a quantum leap forward in the assessment of divergent thinking. The TTCT are probably the longest-running, continually published tests of divergent thinking, the most carefully studied, and the most widely used in educational settings. Indeed, they are almost certainly the most influential creativity assessment yet created. Their influence on creativity research, as noted above, has been immense, and it is not surprising that TTCT scores are commonly used in efficacy studies and meta-analyses of the impact of creativity training programs (e.g., Rose & Lin, 1984).

Over several decades, Torrance refined the administration and scoring of the TTCT, which may account for its enduring popularity. The battery includes Verbal (Thinking Creatively with Words) and Figural tests (Thinking Creatively with Pictures) that each includes a Form A and Form B that can be used alternately. The Figural forms have three subtests:

- *Picture Construction,* in which a participant uses a basic shape and expands on it to create a picture;
- *Picture Completion,* in which a participant is asked to finish and title incomplete drawings; and
- *Lines / Circles,* in which a participant is asked to modify many different series of lines (Form A) or circles (Form B).

The Verbal form has seven subtests. For the first three tasks, the ex-

---

6. Although, oddly enough, in the one direct comparison between the SOI-LA and TTCT-Figural with which we are familiar, the results suggested only a small to moderate overlap among scores (Guillory & Kher-Durlabhji, 1995). This may be due to response set issues (see discussion later in the chapter).

aminee is asked to refer to a picture at the beginning of the test booklet. For example, in Form A, the picture is of an elf staring at its reflection in a pool of water. These first three tasks are considered part of the Ask-and-Guess section:

- *Asking,* in which a participant asks as many questions as possible about the picture;
- *Guessing Causes,* in which a participant lists possible causes for the pictured action;
- *Guessing Consequences,* in which a participant lists possible consequences for the pictured action.

The final four verbal subtests are self-contained:

- *Product Improvement,* in which a participant is asked to make changes to improve a toy (e.g., a stuffed animal)
- *Unusual Uses,* in which a participant is asked to think of many different possible uses for an ordinary item (e.g., a cardboard box)
- *Unusual Questions,* in which a participant asks as many questions as possible about an ordinary item (this item does not appear in later editions); and
- *Just Suppose,* in which a participant is asked to "just suppose" that an improbable situation has happened then list possible ramifications. (See Rapid Reference 2.1.)

Administration, scoring, and score reporting of the various tests and forms are standardized, and detailed norms were created and revised accordingly (see Torrance, 1972b, 1974a; Torrance & Ball, 1984). Although Torrance recommended that scorers be trained, he did find that cursory levels of training (i.e., reading and understanding the scoring manual) allowed novice raters to produce scores associated with acceptable reliability estimates. His one caveat was that untrained raters tend to deviate from the scoring system when assessing originality,

≡ *Rapid Reference 2.1*

Tests and Subtests of the
Torrance Tests of Creative Thinking (TTCT)

Figural		Picture Construction
		Picture Completion
		Lines/Circles
Verbal	Ask-and-Guess	Asking
	Ask-and-Guess	Guessing Causes
	Ask-and-Guess	Guessing Consequences
	Self-Contained	Product Improvement
	Self-Contained	Unusual Uses
	Self-Contained	Unusual Questions
	Self-Contained	Just Suppose

injecting their own personal judgments on the scoring of individual responses.

The original test produced scores in the traditional four DT areas, but the streamlined scoring system introduced in the 1984 revision made significant changes to the available scores. Under the streamlined system, the Figural tests can be scored for resistance to premature closure and abstractness of titles in addition to the familiar scores of fluency, elaboration, and originality. Flexibility was removed because those scores tended to be largely undifferentiated from fluency scores (Hébert, Cramond, Spiers-Neumeister, Millar, & Silvian, 2002).

Resistance to premature closure is determined by an examinee's tendency to not immediately close the incomplete figures on the Figural Picture Completion test. Torrance believed this tendency reflected the examinee's ability "to keep open and delay closure long enough to make the mental leap that makes possible original ideas. Less creative persons tend to leap to conclusions prematurely without considering the available information" (Torrance & Ball, 1984, p. 20). Each response on the Picture Completion task is scored zero points for completing the given figure "by one of the quickest, easiest, most direct routes," one point for completing the figure indirectly, or two points for never completing the figure or doing so "with irregular lines which form part of the picture rather than with straight lines or simple curved lines."

Abstractness of titles is determined by the titles given to objects in the Picture Construction and Picture Completion activities on the Figural test. Torrance and Ball stated that,

> The ability to produce good titles involves the synthesizing and organizing processes of thinking. . . . There is the ability to capture the essence of the information involved, to know what is important. Such a title enables the viewer to see the picture more deeply and richly. (p. 19)

Scores range from zero points for obvious or generic titles (e.g., "Hat" or "Mountains") to one point for simple descriptive titles ("Dancing Cat") to two points for imaginative, descriptive titles that extend beyond concrete descriptions ("The Giant's Finger Puppet") to three points for abstract but appropriate titles that extend beyond the picture and tell a story ("Time of Your Life" or "Season's Change").

Thirteen additional, criterion-referenced scores can be calculated, including emotional expressiveness, synthesis of incomplete figures, internal visualization, richness of imagery, and humor. The Verbal tests can be scored for fluency, originality, and flexibility. Palaniappan and Torrance (2001), using a sample of Malaysian students, found high correlations between the scores in the traditional and streamlined scoring systems.

The voluminous research on the psychometric properties of the Torrance Tests generally provides convincing evidence of reliability and concurrent validity, especially for scores related to the main four DT aspects of fluency, originality, flexibility, and elaboration (e.g., Swartz, 1988; Torrance, 1968, 1974b, 1988; Torrance & Ball, 1984; Treffinger, 1985). However, other evidence of construct validity is less convincing, with factor analytic examinations finding little support for the existence of the proposed score categories. For example, Heausler and Thompson (1988) found evidence for one factor (i.e., a composite score rather than the official scores). The recommendation for using only a composite score for the TTCT is not unprecedented (e.g., Thorndike, 1972), but Kim (2006), among many others, has found evidence for multifaceted factor structures underlying TTCT data; more important, however, is the fact that few of these factor structures appear to support the construct validity of the TTCT.

One possible reason for the construct validity issues is the use of the same participant responses to derive multiple scores (i.e., the "response set" problem; see Heausler & Thompson, 1988; Thorndike, 1972). This type of scoring may lead to the high correlations often found among TTCT scores, which results in researchers finding latent factor structures that do not reflect Torrance's approach to DT assessment. The response set problem appears to be a bigger issue for the TTCT than some other DT assessments, due in large part to the TTCT's scoring system. Indeed, Guilford's empirical approach minimized response set bias, and his work is associated with more positive evaluations of construct validity than the TTCT.

Analysis of TTCT results usually show no overall gender differences in creativity (e.g., Chrisler, 1991; DeSousa Filho & Alencar, 2003; Donnell, 2005; Matud, Rodríguez, & Grande, 2007; Rawashdeh & Al-Qudah, 2003; Saeki, Fan, & Van Dusen, 2001; Ziv, 1980), but girls may report more sexual responses while boys may provide more aggressive responses (Dudek & Verreault, 1989). Strough and Diriwaechter (2000) also found that boys are more likely to report aggressive ideas and less likely to report prosocial responses. Some TTCT studies have suggested that the tests are more predictive of creative behavior in males than females (Arnold & Subotnik, 1994; Cramond, 1994; Howieson, 1981). However, evidence of predictive validity is generally considered to be lacking. This criticism strikes us as a

> **DON'T FORGET**
>
> Most studies have found no gender differences in measures of divergent thinking.

bit unfair, and the actual research in this area is more complex (and more positive) than the conventional wisdom would have us believe. Predictive validity for DT tests as a group is discussed in greater depth near the end of this chapter.

Other DT Assessments

As mentioned earlier, the stark majority of DT assessments are based on, borrowed from, or very similar to the work described previously (e.g., Hu & Adey, 2002; Lin, Hu, Adey, & Shen, 2003; Torrance, 1981; Torrance, Khatena, & Cunnington, 1973; Williams, 1980). For example, the DT scores derived from the Profile of Creative Abilities (Ryser, 2007) are based on Guilford's work and also share some similarities with some TTCT tasks. However, one interesting departure is the use of real-world DT items, which tend to be similar to many of the Guilford and Wallach and Kogan verbal tasks but place the tasks firmly within a realistic, applied context. The rationale for this modification is that a more realistic assessment of applicable DT skills can take place within a realistic context. As Runco (1999) noted, "If divergent thinking tasks are being used in a practical setting . . . , it is probably desirable that the skills or strategies . . . generalize to the natural environment. For this reason realistic divergent thinking tasks might be given."

Runco and his colleagues have developed a number of these realistic DT tasks and gathered evidence of adequate reliability (Chand & Runco, 1993). For example, Plucker, Runco, and Lim (2006) used the following two tasks, which were adapted from Chand and Runco and scored for fluency and originality.

Your friend Pat sits next to you in class. Pat really likes to talk to you and often bothers you while you are doing your work. Sometimes he distracts you and you miss an important part of the lecture, and many times you don't finish your work because he is bothering you. What should you do? How would you solve this problem? Remember to list as many ideas and solutions as you can.

It's a great day for sailing, and your friend, Kelly, asks you if you want to go sailing. Unfortunately, you have a big project due tomorrow, and it requires a full day to complete. You would rather be sailing. What are you going to do? Think of as many ideas as you can.

Other DT tests are domain specific; one such example is the Creative Engineering Design Assessment or CEDA (Charyton, Jagacinski, Merrill & Lilly, in press). The CEDA model is based on past research on creative processes in engineering design that are domain specific (Cropley & Cropley, 2005; Nickerson, 1999; Stokes, 2005). Results suggest that engineering design creativity may be a specialized skill that needs to be honed in engineering students.

Remote Associates Test

Another assessment that is generally assumed to tap into DT skills, yet is quite different from the traditional DT tests described earlier in this chapter, is the Remote Associates Test (Mednick, 1968). This test was based on associative theory, with the premise that "creative thinking . . . consists of the forming of mutually distant associative elements into new combinations which are useful and meet specified as well as unforeseen requirements" (p. 213). In other words, more creative individuals are assumed to be able to make meaningful, useful associations between disparate concepts and ideas to a greater extent than a relatively uncre-

> **DON'T FORGET**
>
> The Remote Associates Test looks for the ability to make associations between disparate concepts.

ative individual (see also Mednick, 1962). The resulting assessment, the Remote Associates Test or RAT, consists of 30 items. Each item includes three stimulus words, with the instruction to find a fourth word that links the entire pool of stimuli. Mednick (1968) provides the following example: wheel, electric, high. Potential scoring responses would be chair or wire. Although reliability evidence for the RAT is satisfactory (Mednick, 1968), evidence of validity is mixed or lacking (Fasko, 1999). There have been several updates to the original Remote Associates Test that modify out-of-date language and phrases (e.g., Bowers, Regehr, Balthazard, & Parker, 1990; Kihlstrom, Shames, & Dorfman, 1996; Smith & Blankenship, 1991). One such revision (Kihlstrom et al., 1996), with 68 items, is available for free on the Internet at http://socrates.berkeley.edu/~kihlstrm/RATest.htm. There typically have been no gender differences found on the RAT (Chusmir & Koberg, 1986; Harris, 2004), although one study found that females scored higher (Richardson, 1985).

ADMINISTRATION

A great deal of research has focused on the impact of various administration strategies on subsequent performance. Much of this work is summarized quite effectively by Torrance (1988) and will only be briefly reviewed here. He noted that explicit instructions to be original (e.g., Try to think of a picture no one else will think of, which is taken directly from the TTCT), warm-up activities, providing cue-rich environments, and either relaxed (game-like) or slightly stressful conditions tend to produce higher DT scores than other tested conditions, although this research is not unequivocal. Subsequent research is largely consistent with the 1988 summary on administration conditions, although Runco, Illies, and Reiter-Palmon (2005) recently conducted an interesting administration study. They compared the impact of two different types of explicit instructions on DT test performance. Runco et al., among other experimental manipulations, differentiated between process-focused instructions (think of things that will be thought of by no one else) and content-focused instructions (be original). Results suggest that process-focused instructions have a greater impact, especially on originality scores.

SCORING

Traditional strategies for scoring DT tests are straightforward. Fluency is nearly always a direct count of the number of responses to a particular prompt or task. Originality is usually interpreted as a measure of statistical infrequency, which Guilford referred to as cleverness. The tests reviewed above either created large norming samples from which statistical infrequency was calculated or manipulate the total response pool so that a given percent of responses are scored as original. For example, Plucker, Runco, and Lim (2006) scored their total response pool so that roughly 10 percent of the students' ideas were scored as original. Flexibility is generally based on the number of categories or classes represented in a respondent's pool of ideas. For example, in response to "List things that have wheels," a response pool of "cars, watches, Swiss cheese makers" would be scored as more flexible than "bicycles, tricycles, scooters." Elaboration, which is a much less common score in the research literature, involves the degree to which respondents have gone beyond the anticipated norm with regard to detail on a particular prompt or task. For example, on the TTCT Figural form, participants are given extra points for each detail they add to the first task. A student who adds 20–30 extra details to the picture will be scored much higher on elaboration than a student who adds a couple details.

However, recent analyses of various scoring systems provide evidence that alternatives to the traditional scores should be considered. These alternatives include the calculation of summative scores (i.e., totaling fluency, flexibility, and originality scores), highly uncommon scores (answers given by less than 5 percent of participants), weighted fluency scores, percentage scores, and scores based upon the entire body of each subject's answers as opposed to scoring individual responses in a list of ideas (Hocevar & Michael, 1979; Runco & Charles, 1993; Runco & Mraz, 1992; Runco, Okuda, & Thurston, 1987).

Subjective Evaluation of DT Test Results

Some recent attention has focused on evaluation of responses by external judges or the respondents themselves, with a complex pattern of results. For example, Grohman, Wodniecka, and Klusak (2006) found evidence that, when judging the uniqueness of ideas, those individuals with high DT skills tend to underestimate the uniqueness of ideas of others. Conversely, overall DT performance correlated positively with intrapersonal evaluation of uniqueness. These results extend previous research suggesting that people have greater difficulty evaluating highly original ideas than less original ideas (Runco & Chand, 1994; Runco & Smith, 1992; Runco & Vega, 1990; cf. to Charles & Runco, 2000–2001); Blair and Mumford (2007) go so far as to conclude that "people have a marked disdain for original and risky ideas" (p. 216), probably due to an aversion to ideas that are inconsistent with societal norms and mores.

Mumford and his colleagues have proposed a model of the cognition of idea evaluation, with promising results in initial empirical studies (Licuanan, Dailey, & Mumford, 2007; Lonergan, Scott, & Mumford,

2004). Collectively, this research suggests that the use of subjective judgments—by self or others—of DT items and response pools may hold promise as an alternative scoring strategy, but that raters may tend to underestimate originality if steps are not taken to help correct this bias.[7]

Fluency as a Contaminating Factor

Several researchers have noted that fluency can be a contaminating influence on originality scores—if fluency is controlled, reliability evidence for originality scores is often very poor (Clark & Mirels, 1970; Hocevar, 1979c, 1979d; Seddon, 1983). But this work has significant empirical (Runco & Albert, 1985) and theoretical limitations (e.g., the possible role of associative hierarchies in creative individuals, see Mednick, 1962; Milgram & Rabkin, 1980). A case in point is the effort by Runco and Albert (1985) to utilize both verbal and nonverbal tasks, since Hocevar (1979a, 1979c) only used verbal tests. Runco and Albert found that originality scores produced evidence of reliability after removing fluency effects on the nonverbal tasks, with significant differences among groups based on achievement (i.e., gifted vs. non-gifted students).

Snyder, Mitchell, Bossomaier, and Pallier (2004) proposed the calculation of a Creativity Quotient (CQ), a unique statistical solution for the fluency problem. Their formula rewards response pools that are highly fluent but also highly flexible. The formula is represented in the following form, with N_c representing the number of distinct categories in a given pool of responses (i.e., a fairly traditional definition of

---

7. Runco (in press) pointed out that subjective self-ratings involve both divergent and convergent skills, yet there is reason to believe these are very different sets of skills, confounding any results that emerge from self-rating approaches.

flexibility), and n_2 representing "the number of distinctly different categories for which at least two suggested uses were given," n_3 the number of categories for which three uses were given, and so on.[8]

CAUTION

Fluency may have a particularly large effect on originality scores.

$$CQ = N_c + \frac{1}{2}n_2 + \frac{1}{3}n_3 + \frac{1}{4}n_4 \ldots$$

The practical effect of the formula is that the CQ increases by 1 the first time an idea from a category is provided; the second instance increases the CQ by a half point; the third increases the CQ by only a third point, and on and on. The authors give the example of two response pools: In the first, seven ideas are provided within the same category, leading to a CQ of approximately 3. In the second, seven ideas are provided in seven distinct categories, providing a CQ of 7. Psychometric evidence in support of the use of CQ is currently lacking, but it provides a good example of the types of statistical manipulations being attempted in order to address fluency's role in DT scores. See Snyder et al. (2004) for a more detailed explanation of the development of the CQ formula.

Although several suggestions have been made regarding techniques for removing the influence of fluency on originality (e.g., Clark & Mirels, 1970, Hocevar, 1979a, 1979b; Hocevar & Michael, 1979), few studies have evaluated and compared the various suggestions with respect to the reliability and validity evidence for resulting originality scores. For example, researchers have suggested that DT tests be administered so

---

8. See Snyder et al. (2004) for a more detailed explanation of the development of the CQ formula.

that every person provides the same number of answers, that originality scores be subjectively determined by external raters, that percentage scoring formulas be used, or that some combination of these techniques be employed (Clark & Mirels, 1970; Hocevar, 1979a; Hocevar & Michael, 1979; Runco & Mraz, 1992). Additionally, the possibility that individuals can subjectively rate the originality of their own responses has yet to be investigated in this context (cf. Runco & Smith, 1992).

Perhaps most importantly, the relative impact of these methods on concurrent validity has not been examined. Hocevar and Michael (1979) correctly observed that a majority of psychometric studies of DT test scores concentrated on obtaining evidence of reliability and convergent validity, while little evidence was gathered of discriminant validity. Consequently, subsequent research attempted to answer the discriminant validity questions but overlooked issues related to convergent validity (i.e., How do the various techniques for controlling for fluency impact correlations between DT originality scores and external criteria of creativity?) and more practical issues (i.e., How do each of the various techniques impact who is admitted to gifted and talented programs?). Although Runco and his colleagues (e.g., Runco, 1985; Runco & Mraz, 1992; Runco, Okuda, & Thurston, 1987) have conducted several studies to investigate the impact of various DT scoring techniques, similar studies explicitly comparing techniques for controlling fluency have yet to be published (although we know of several that are nearing completion or in press). Issues of convergent validity need to be addressed in order for us to gain a comprehensive understanding of the impact of fluency on originality.

However, one question remains to be asked: Is it really so bad that fluency is a contaminating factor? In the real world, do we penalize someone who comes up with a great solution to a problem just because she or he came up with a lot of ideas while trying to identify potential solutions? Indeed, research by Dean Simonton has found that sheer quantity of output is a strong predictor of quality in both composers

(1977) and psychologists (1985). Two-time Nobel Prize winner Linus Pauling once said, "The best way to get a good idea is to get a lot of ideas."

Given that the foundation of divergent thinking is essentially ideational fluency, one could be forgiven for asking if contamination by fluency should be receiving so much attention.[9] Indeed, Wallach and Wing (1969) provide evidence that fluency is a better predictor of some outcomes than originality. They also note the numerous studies that find ideas later in a list to be more original than those early in a list.

So how should someone interested in DT testing proceed? Collectively, the work cited above suggests that the role of fluency is more complex than originally thought, and the possible—but by no means assured—contamination effect of fluency should be considered when scoring (and planning to score) responses to DT tasks.

THE PARTICULAR PROBLEM OF PREDICTIVE VALIDITY

As noted above, the most widely used DT tests are arguably associated with evidence of reliability and concurrent validity. However, the perceived lack of predictive validity (Baer, 1993a, 1993b, 1994b, 1994c; Gardner, 1988, 1993; Kogan & Pankove, 1974; Weisberg, 1993) has led researchers and educators to avoid the use of these tests and continues to serve as a lightning rod for criticisms of the psychometric study of creativity (Plucker & Renzulli, 1999).

Taylor and Holland (1964) recommended longitudinal studies that "use a very wide variety of potential predictors, and then, after a suitable follow-up period, utilize good external criteria of creativity" (p.

---

9. We acknowledge that the high correlations between fluency and originality scores may be a cause of the weak construct validity evidence, but the response set problem and controlling for fluency when scoring originality are related but not identical issues.

48) in order to collect evidence of creativity measures' predictive validity. Yet just over a decade later, in an evaluation of efforts to establish DT tests' predictive validity, Wallach (1976) stated that "subjects vary widely and systematically in their attainments—yet little if any of that systematic variation is captured by individual differences on ideational fluency tests" (p. 60).

Although the possibility exists that DT tests simply lack predictive validity, researchers have suggested several possible reasons for divergent thinking tests' apparent weakness in this area. A majority of the possible reasons represent weaknesses in methodology more than weaknesses in the psychometric integrity of DT tests. A summary of these arguments is presented in Table 2.2. Researchers who have addressed at least a few of these weaknesses (e.g., domain specific studies by Ignatz, 1982, and Sawyers & Canestaro, 1989) have collected positive evidence of predictive validity (e.g., Hong, Milgram, & Gorsky, 1995; Milgram & Hong, 1993; Okuda, Runco, & Berger, 1991; Plucker, 1999).

Another methodological factor that may have a negative impact on the predictive validity of DT test scores is the reliance on ineffective outcome criteria in longitudinal studies. For example, Runco (1986a) stressed that both quantity and quality of creative achievement should be included as outcome variables, in contrast to a traditional reliance on quantity. Again, studies including both types of outcome variables provide considerably improved support for the predictive validity of DT tests (e.g., Plucker, 1999). Runco has developed a criterion measure that is directly related to ideation, which he feels is what DT should predict, as opposed to, for instance, achievement in crafts or some verbal domain (Runco, Plucker, & Lim, 2000–2001; see related discussion in Chapter 5).

However, and this is a very important caveat, the poor predictive power of divergent thinking tests is not universally accepted. To the contrary, several studies provide at least limited evidence of discriminant and predictive validity for DT tests (Howieson, 1981; Milgram

Table 2.2 Methodological Issues in Studies of DT Tests' Predictive Validity

- Scores may be susceptible to various coaching, training, and intervention effects (Clapham, 1996; Feldhusen & Clinkenbeard, 1986; Hattie, 1980; Torrance, 1972a, 1988).

- Administration conditions (e.g., game-like vs. test-like, timed vs. untimed, individual vs. group) appear to influence originality and fluency scores (Chand & Runco, 1992; Renzulli, Owen, & Callahan, 1974; Runco, 1986c; Runco & Okuda, 1991; Torrance, 1971; Wallach, 1976).

- Longitudinal studies may be too brief to allow people to achieve creatively (Torrance, 1972b, 1979).

- Studies may overemphasize quantity of creative achievement at the expense of quality of achievement (Runco, 1986b).

- Statistical procedures may be inadequate for the analysis of complex longitudinal data (Hocevar & Bachelor, 1989; Plucker & Renzulli, 1999).

- Homogeneity of the sample with respect to achievement or ability may influence results, since somewhat improved psychometric properties are generally associated with samples of gifted or high-achieving children (Runco, 1985, 1986b; Runco & Albert, 1985; see Runco, 1986a, for an exception).

- Initial socioeconomic conditions and intervening life events may make prediction of adult creative achievement primarily on the basis of ideational thinking test scores difficult (Cramond, 1993, 1994; Torrance, 1981b).

- Score distributions are often nonnormally distributed, violating the assumptions of many statistical procedures (Hocevar & Bachelor, 1989; Plucker & Renzulli, 1999; Torrance, 1979).

- Creative achievement in adulthood may be domain specific, yet the predictor measures are almost universally domain general (Plucker & Renzulli, 1999).

CAUTION

The predictive validity of Divergent Thinking tests is a highly debated area.

& Hong, 1994; Milgram & Milgram, 1976; Okuda, Runco, & Berger, 1991; Rotter, Langland, & Berger, 1971; Runco, 1986a; Torrance, 1969, 1972a, 1972b, 1981a, 1981b; Torrance & Safter, 1989; Torrance, Tan, & Allman, 1970; Torrance & Wu, 1981; Yamada & Tam, 1996). As noted earlier, the evidence becomes even more positive under certain sampling and assessment conditions recommended in the literature (e.g., samples of high IQ children, utilizing content specific DT measures; see Clapham, Cowdery, King, & Montang, 2005; Hocevar, 1981; Ignatz, 1982; Milgram & Milgram, 1976; Runco, 1986b).

An interesting wrinkle in the predictive validity research is that evidence of predictive validity is generally stronger for boys than girls (e.g., Howieson 1981; Ignatz, 1982; Torrance, 1981). Why this is often the case is yet to be explained, but this phenomenon should be kept in mind during score interpretation.

DEMOGRAPHIC DIFFERENCES

Torrance (1970; Torrance & Myers, 1971) strongly believed that creative teaching was a key strategy for improving educational outcomes and life experiences for disadvantaged students, and Runco (1993a) has expressed similar sentiments. This begs the question of whether demographic differences exist on DT tests.

Numerous studies report few if any significant differences between white and black students in creative production, creative thinking, training of creativity, or the relationship between intelligence and creativity, and DT tests are no exception (e.g., Glover, 1976; Iscoe & Pierce-Jones, 1964; Kaltsounis, 1974; Knox & Glover, 1978; Torrance, 1971a, 1973). However, research on white-Hispanic differences in creativity has produced mixed results (e.g., Garcia, 2003, among others).

Indeed, some of the only differences tend to favor black students. Torrance (1971, 1973) found that black children scored higher on the TTCT than white children on the Figural tests in fluency, flexibility, and originality, and white students scored higher on Figural elaboration and all Verbal subtests. However, the differences were significantly reduced when the scores of black and white students of similar socioeconomic status were compared.

Comparisons of DT scores of Hispanic and white students tend to find different results depending on whether the creativity measure is verbal or nonverbal. For example, Argulewicz and Kush (1984) found that white children scored higher than Hispanic children on three of four TTCT Verbal tasks but found no significant differences on the Figural tasks. Studies using only non-verbal assessments have typically found no differences (e.g., Argulewicz, Elliott, & Hall, 1982) or show a slight advantage for bilingual Hispanic students (Kessler & Quinn, 1987; Price-Williams & Ramirez, 1971).

Studies utilizing the TTCT often show people in Western cultures outperforming people in Eastern cultures, reflecting the conventional wisdom among creativity researchers (see Kaufman & Sternberg, 2006). Research provides evidence that American college students score higher on the TTCT than Japanese college students (Saeki, Fan, & Van Dusen, 2001), and that Americans across five different age groups score higher than their peers in Hong Kong (Jaquish & Ripple, 1984). However, a study by Rudowicz, Lok, and Kitto (1995) suggests that national differences may be more complex. They found that children in Hong Kong scored higher on the TTCT-Figural than children in Taiwan, Singapore, and America, but lower than German children. However, results from the TTCT-Verbal showed the exact opposite pattern. Other studies on Asians or Asian Americans included Pornrungroj (1992), who gave the Figural form of the TTCT to Thai children and Thai-American children and found Thai children received significantly higher scores than did Thai Americans, and Yoon (2006), who gave the TTCT to

European-American and Asian-American middle school students (the latter being a mix of Chinese American, Korean American, Japanese American, and Southeastern Asian Americans). Yoon found no significant differences either between the European American and Asian Americans or between the different subgroups of Asian Americans.

IS THERE A FOURTH-GRADE SLUMP?

Torrance (1962, 1965, 1968), as a result of his numerous cross-sectional and longitudinal studies, discovered that students' TTCT scores decreased for a high percentage of students in fourth grade yet rebounded almost completely by fifth grade (completely in the cases of originality and elaboration). Other researchers and theorists (e.g., Gardner, 1980) perceive a longer general decline in creative performance through the late elementary grades. Possible causes include socialization and changes in school climate as students enter the later elementary grades, although success in correcting the effects of the slump through focused classroom treatment (Torrance & Gupta, 1964) suggest the latter cause.

Unfortunately, decreases in ideational thinking performance in the middle to late elementary grades have been the subject of few significant research efforts in the last 20 years, and these investigations produced conflicting results (e.g., Johnson, 1985; Torrance, 1967). For example, Wu, Cheng, Ip, and McBride-Chang (2005) found that Grade 6 students outperformed university students on TTCT figural and verbal tasks, yet on an applied, real-world task, university students outperformed the young adolescents. Claxton, Pannells, and Rhoads (2005) found an even more complex pattern of results as students moved from Grade 4 to Grade 9, with the students scoring highest in Grade 4, lowest in Grade 6, and by Grade 9 they had returned to similar but slightly lower levels as occurred in Grade 4 (with the exception of elaboration, which increased at each milestone). At this point, it seems safest to conclude that variations in DT test performance exist as people develop, but there is no consensus on when, how much, or why, although we have some decent guesses (i.e., at some point in late elementary school; not very big; for lots of possible reasons, many of them social).[10]

LIMITATIONS

As with any assessment, divergent thinking measures have a number of important limitations, many of which have already been described. For example, the tests are susceptible to administration and training effects; some of the measures, especially those only loosely based on the SOI and TTCT approaches, have questionable psychometric quality; and the scores tend to tempt people to overgeneralize DT test performance to all other aspects of creativity.

With this last point in mind, the predominance of divergent thinking in creativity research probably devalues the integral role of creativity in the solving of problems. Professing a viewpoint widely held by other researchers (e.g., Basadur, Wakabayashi, & Graen, 1990; Mumford, 2003; Osborn, 1963; Parnes, Noller, & Biondi, 1977; Simonton, 1988b; Torrance, 1976), Runco (1991) observes, "the evaluative component of the creative process has received very little attention. This is surprising because it is a vital constituent of the creative process, and is required whenever an individual selects or expresses a preference for an idea or set of ideas" (p. 312). The movement toward psychometric research involving aspects of creative problem solving other than divergent production, such as problem identification (Runco & Okuda, 1988; Wakefield, 1985) and evaluative thinking (Okuda, Runco, & Berger,

---

10. For further reading on the relationship between creativity and developmental progression in education, see Kaufman and Baer (2006).

1991; Runco, 1991; Runco & Chand, 1994), is gathering steam, but the psychometric application of this work is still in its infancy.

All of this makes us wonder if the historical focus on divergent thinking tests among academics and educators has had a generally negative effect on the influence of the field of creativity as a whole. After all, it is worrisome to read comprehensive reviews of research on human cognition or problem solving (e.g., Davidson & Sternberg, 2003; Sternberg, 1999b) and see hardly any mention of divergent thinking (or hardly any mention of creativity outside of the occasional creativity chapter). As classically defined, is divergent thinking a passé construct?

We think not—but with several caveats. First, it is incumbent on creativity researchers interested in DT to make a stronger case for the present-day relevancy of divergent thinking. Mumford (2003) conceptualizes divergent thinking as encompassing a wide range of skills and abilities, including problem finding, information gathering, conceptual combination, and idea generation. This approach strikes us as a good start. Few people simply describe cognition as thinking, and similarly describing divergent thinking as "thinking of many ideas"—in other words, ideational fluency—is equally restrictive and psychologically limiting.

Second, the classic DT assessments may gain wider acceptance and use if they were revised to include a greater emphasis on domain specificity. A straightforward example is provided by Hu and Adey's (2002) Scientific Creativity Test for Secondary Students, which modifies classic DT tasks to add a science focus. For example, Item 1 is a variation of the traditional unusual uses task: "Please write down as many as possible scientific uses as you can for a piece of glass"; Item 3, a product improvement task, asks students to "Please think up as many possible improvements as you can to a regular bicycle, making it more interesting, more useful, and more beautiful." In addition to the potential for greater evidence of predictive validity, domain specific assessment approaches will better reflect the direction of learning and cognitive science research than the current, domain general approach (Kaufman & Baer, 2005).[11]

Third, DT assessments should more directly address the response set problem that plagues factor analytic studies of these measures' construct validity. Creating administration and scoring techniques that minimize response set bias and provide evidence of distinct DT score categories should be possible, but little effort has been expended in this area. Doing so could potentially—and only potentially—address one of the major criticisms of DT tests, especially the TTCT.

Fourth, divergent thinking research and assessment would greatly benefit from a greater emphasis on utility of ideation creativity (Plucker et al., 2004; Runco & Charles, 1993; Runco et al., 2005). Creativity is more than fluency or novelty; usefulness is a key component of creativity—a component neglected when one relies solely on the traditional divergent thinking measures to estimate creativity. Although there have been recent suggestions that subjective scoring techniques may be the most effective way to determine usefulness (Silvia et al., in press), research on objective scoring of usefulness provides convincing evidence that (a) it can be done and (b) it can be done well (Runco & Charles, 1993; Runco & Mraz, 1992; Runco et al., 2005).

One way researchers have ensured usefulness is a part of the creative process is to analyze problem-solving processes. An example of problem solving and the creativity process is the study of insight. Insight, or the moment of understanding or comprehension, is how individuals solve problems. Research on insight has been becoming common (e.g., Dominowski & Dallob, 1995; Finke, 1995; Martinsen, 1993, 1995) and insight has been referred to as the most important cognitive pro-

---

11. Admittedly a controversial point, but only mildly so. See, for example, Baer (1998), Plucker (1998), and Plucker (2005).

≡ *Rapid Reference 2.2*

Improving Divergent Thinking Tests

Four ways that divergent thinking assessments might be improved include:

- Current DT researchers should make a better case for their relevancy today.
- DT tests should become more domain-specific to reflect the growing tendency toward both domain-specific and domain-general measures.
- DT tests should create better administration and scoring techniques that minimize response set bias and provide evidence of distinct DT score categories.

cess (Pretz & Totz, 2007). Other promising areas include the evaluative work of Runco and his colleagues (e.g., Runco, 1992b). (See Rapid Reference 2.2.)

CONCLUSIONS AND RECOMMENDATIONS

Runco's (1993b) response to criticisms of the study of divergent thinking strike us as appropriate to the current situation:

> Theorists who dismiss divergent thinking as entirely unimportant have ignored recent empirical research. . . . Additionally, some critics seem to expect too much from divergent thinking. Again, divergent thinking is not synonymous with creativity. Divergent thinking tests are, however, very useful estimates of the potential for creative thought. Although a high score on a divergent thinking test does not guarantee outstanding performance in the natural environment, these tests do lead to useful predictions about

who is capable of such performances. . . . [D]ivergent thinking is a predictor of original thought, not a criterion of creative ability. (p. 16)

When assessing creativity, using DT in isolation simply does not make a lot of sense. It made sense in the early 1970s, but several decades later we have much more complex systems theories of creativity that raise other factors to the exalted heights that DT once occupied alone. Even if studying creative cognition, the richness of creativity should be acknowledged by using a variety of instruments to reflect the diverse processes that contribute to creative cognition.

However, if one is interested in studying and/or assessing only divergent thinking, the voluminous research on DT task administration should be considered during DT test administration, scoring, and interpretation. As we noted throughout this chapter, administration and scoring strategies for DT tests can have profound differences on the quality of information gathered and the ability to interpret those scores meaningfully.

Finally, in addition to relying on broader definitions of DT as recommended in the previous sections, we recommend that users of DT tests and consumers of their data keep in mind that other scores can be calculated in addition to fluency and originality. In fact, an argument can be made that flexibility, if not also elaboration, is perhaps the most important aspect of DT (e.g., Chi, 1997).

🍂 TEST YOURSELF 🍂

1. **Which one of the following is *not* a key component of divergent thinking?**

   (a) Fluency

   (b) Elaboration

   (c) Integration

2. **The Structure of Intellect model looks at both the types of content and the types of product in divergent thinking.** True or False?

3. **Wallach and Kogan have argued that divergent thinking tasks should be administered in what type of atmosphere?**

   (a) Serious

   (b) Fast-paced

   (c) Game-like

4. **The most commonly used divergent thinking tasks were developed by:**

   (a) Wallach and Kogan

   (b) Torrance

   (c) Guilford

5. **The Remote Associates Test offers three different words, and test-takers are asked to:**

   (a) Suggest what they all have in common

   (b) Find a fourth word that is linked with all three

   (c) Pick out the word that doesn't belong

6. **Which component of divergent thinking may have a particularly large effect?**

   (a) Originality

   (b) Fluency

   (c) Mindfulness

7. **Some studies have shown that creativity tends to decline in:**

   (a   College

   (b) One's forties

   (c) Fourth grade

Answers: 1. c; 2. True; 3. c; 4. b; 5. b; 6. b; 7. c

Three

THE CONSENSUAL ASSESSMENT TECHNIQUE

Why do you believe that Picasso's *Guernica* is a creative painting? Why do you think Mozart was more creative than Salieri? And how would you judge the creativity of some recent eleven-dimensional string theories?

You may have expertise in one (or if you are a Renaissance person, possibly even two) of those three areas, but it is highly likely that in making at least one of these three judgments you don't really feel qualified to make a response you would feel confident in defending. And even though you might know enough about, say, the works of Mozart and Salieri to give an informed opinion, does your opinion "count" as much as the opinions of recognized experts in the field?

These considerations raise an important question: How is creativity at the highest levels judged? It isn't based on a procedure that awards points for different attributes of a painting, composition, or theory. There is no test to determine which philosopher's theories, which biologist's models, or which dramatist's plays are the most creative. Nobel Prize committees don't apply rubrics, complete checklists, or score tests. What do they do? They ask experts. The best assessment of the creativity in any field is usually the collective judgment of recognized experts in that field. It is certainly true that experts from different eras may come to different conclusions (and pity the poor artists and scientists whose genius is only recognized when it is too late for them to enjoy their posthumous fame). However, many argue that the best assessment one can make of the creativity of anyone's theories, artworks, compositions, or other creations is the overall judgment of experts in their field.

Such an emphasis on the creative product may seem like it is giving short shrift to the other Four P's (person, process, and press), but it is consistent with years of creativity theory. MacKinnon (1978) stated that "the starting point, indeed the bedrock of all studies of creativity, is an analysis of creative products, a determination of what it is that makes them different from more mundane products" (p. 187). He is only one of many to value the creative product (e.g., Besemer & Treffinger, 1981; Ghiselin, 1963; Guilford, 1957; Jackson & Messick, 1965; Taylor, 1960; Treffinger & Poggio, 1972; Wallach, 1976). Runco (1989b) argued that evaluating creative products may address measurement problems caused by the inconsistent psychometric quality of divergent thinking tests.

Indeed, such an emphasis on the creative product emerged in response to perceived needs for external criteria to which researchers could compare other methods of assessing creativity to help establish evidence of validity. However, an absolute and indisputable criterion of creativity is not readily available (there is no one, single magic number or test), hence the *criterion problem* (McPherson, 1963; Shapiro, 1970).

There are several approaches to evaluating the creative product. There are, for example, several straightforward rating scales (Besemer & O'Quin, 1993; Hargreaves, Galton, & Robinson, 1996; Treffinger, 1989). Teacher ratings receive a lot of attention in educational circles, with key work being accomplished by Besemer and O'Quin (1986; O'Quin & Besemer, 1989), Reis and Renzulli (1991), Westberg (1991), and Runco (Runco, 1984, 2002; Runco, Johnson, and Bear, 1993) during the last two decades. Each of these instruments asks educators to rate specific aspects of students' creative products. For example, the Creative Product Semantic Scale (Besemer & O'Quin, 1993) has raters evaluate the novelty, problem resolution, and elaboration and synthesis attributes of products, whereas the Student Product Assessment Form

(Reis & Renzulli, 1991) is designed to be an evaluation instrument for gifted programs and provides ratings of nine creative product traits (e.g., problem focusing, appropriateness of resources, originality, action orientation, audience). Westberg (1991) created an instrument to evaluate student inventions, with analyses producing evidence of originality, technical goodness, and aesthetic appeal factors. Runco (1984) developed the Teachers' Evaluation of Student's Creativity (TESC) using adjectives derived from extensive teacher input.

Each of these instruments is associated with evidence of reliability, although validity issues remain to be addressed. In one comparison of teachers' and parents' ability to evaluate children's ideas, the two groups were similarly successful, with a number of children and adult divergent thinking test scores positively and moderately correlated with evaluative skill (Runco & Vega, 1990). Runco et al. (1993) found that teachers and parents shared implicit views of children's creativity (although there was less agreement on what constituted a lack of creativity). Yet composite scores on the TESC and the Parental Evaluation of Student's Creativity (PESC) were not highly correlated (Runco, 1989a).

Although these methods are certainly well used, the most popular way of assessing products is with the Consensual Assessment Technique (CAT). The CAT is based on this idea that the best measure of the creativity of a work of art, a theory, or any other artifact is the combined assessment of experts in that field. Whether one is selecting a poem for a prestigious award or judging the creativity of a fifth grader's collage, one doesn't score it by following some checklist or applying a general creativity-assessment rubric. The best judgments of the creativity of such artifacts that can be produced—imperfect though these may be—are the combined opinions of experts in the field. That's what most prize committees do (which is why only the opinions of a few experts matter when choosing, say, the winner of the Fields Medal in mathematics—the opinions of the rest of us just don't count). The CAT uses essentially the same procedure to judge the creativity of more everyday creations.

The idea of using experts to rate creative products has been around for a long time (e.g., MacKinnon, 1962); one example is when Csikszentmihalyi and Getzels (1971) asked artists and art critics to rate drawings by art students on the basis of craftsmanship, originality, and aesthetic value, with mixed reliability and validity results. Yet the CAT as it is traditionally used today created by Teresa Amabile (1982, 1996) and this particular method has been used extensively in creativity research. Because (a) it is based on actual creative performances or artifacts; (b) it is not tied to any particular theory of creativity[1]; and (c) it mimics the way creativity is assessed in the "real world," the CAT has sometimes been called the "gold standard" of creativity assessment (Carson, 2006). The CAT relies on comparisons of levels of creativity within a group, however, and has no anchors that extend beyond the group of products being compared. Because it does not lend itself to standardized scoring in a way that will allow comparisons to be made across settings, the CAT has seen little use in the individual assessment of creativity. Its widest use is in research, although it can also be used for such school-based tasks as selecting highly creative students for special programs. Examples of such programs that use expert ratings of creative performance include the Governor's School of the Arts or Saint Mary's Center of Creative Problem Solving; admissions to specialized, arts-centered schools as Julliard; and several gifted and talented programs, such as those in the

> **DON'T FORGET**
>
> The Consensual Assessment Technique uses appropriate experts to judge creative products.

---

1. It is important to note that this concept is not universally agreed upon. Others have argued that its atheoretical basis is not a strength, but rather a weakness.

Washington County, Maryland, district (Baer & McKool, in press). As will be discussed in more detail in Chapter Six, Sternberg (2006; see also Sternberg & the Rainbow Project Collaborators, 2006) has included a CAT-like task as a non-required component of admissions to Tufts University.

DESCRIPTION OF THE CAT

When using the CAT, subjects are asked to create something (an actual product) and experts are then asked to evaluate the creativity of those products. The experts work independently and do not influence one another's judgments in any way. Poems, collages, and stories have been widely used in CAT studies, and the potential range of creative products that might work using the CAT is quite wide. In the CAT, rather than try to measure some skill, attribute, or disposition that is theoretically linked to creativity, it is the actual creativity of things subjects have produced that is assessed. The focus is on creative products, not whatever creativity-relevant skills individuals may have or processes they may employ that might lead to creative performance. It is the performance itself that is of interest. As Csikszentmihalyi (1999) wrote, "If creativity is to have a useful meaning, it must refer to a process that results in an idea or product that is recognized and adopted by others. Originality, freshness of perception, divergent-thinking ability are all well and good in their own right, as desirable personal traits. But without some sort of public recognition they do not constitute creativity. . . . The underlying assumption [in all creativity tests] is that an objective quality called 'creativity' is revealed in the products, and that judges and raters can recognize it" (p. 314). Rather than try to measure things that might be associated with creativity or that might be predictive of creativity, the CAT goes right to the heart of creativity by looking at the creative (or not-so-creative) products that subjects have produced.

The basic CAT procedure is to provide subjects with basic instructions for creating some kind of product and then to have a panel of experts, each working independently of one another, assess the creativity of those artifacts. For example, in one study "students were given a line drawing of a girl and a boy . . . [and] asked to write an original story in which the boy and the girl played some part" (Baer, 1994a, p. 39). Experts in the area of children's writing were then asked to rate the creativity of the stories on 1.0-to-5.0 scale. (The range of the scale is a matter of choice, but should have at least three score points so that there can be some diversity of ratings. Typically judges are free to use fractions if they choose—e.g., a judge might give a creativity rating of 4.5—but few judges actually employ fractions.) These expert judges are *not* asked to explain or defend their ratings in any way. They are simply asked to use their expert sense of what is creative in the domain in question to rate the creativity of the products in relation to one another. That is, the ratings can be compared only within the pool of artifacts being judged by a particular panel of experts. High or low levels of creativity, as revealed by the CAT, refer to differences within the group of artifacts judged, not in comparison to any external standard. (See Rapid Reference 3.1.)

≡ Rapid Reference 3.1

Overview of the Consensual Assessment Technique (CAT)

- Is based on the way creativity is judged in the real world
- Expert judges compare actual products created by subjects
- Can only be used for comparisons within the group of artifacts judged by one group of judges
- No standardized scores, only comparative scoring
- Used widely in creativity research, less widely in school settings

RELIABILITY

Inter-rater reliability using the CAT is typically estimated using Cronbach's coefficient alpha, the Spearman-Brown prediction formula, or the intraclass correlation method. These methods generally yield similar inter-rater reliability estimates. In a series of 21 studies of artistic (collage-making) and verbal (poetry-writing and storytelling) creativity that she reported in 1983, Amabile found inter-rater reliabilities ranging from .72 to .93 using the Spearman-Brown prediction formula. In her more recent work (Amabile, 1996) she has found a similar range of inter-rater reliability correlations (from .70 to .89) using Cronbach's coefficient alpha and the intraclass correlation method. Other researchers have generally reported similar inter-rater reliabilities among expert judges, typically in the .70-to-.90 range (e.g., Baer, 1993, 1997, 1998b; Baer, Kaufman, & Gentile, 2004; Conti, Coon, & Amabile, 1996; Hennessey, 1994; Kaufman, Baer, Cole, & Sexton, in press; Runco, 1989b). Generally speaking, the greater the number of judges the higher the overall inter-rater reliability correlations. The average number of expert judges reported by Amabile (1996) in the previously cited studies was just over 10, with a low of 2 (in which case only a simple r correlation coefficient could be reported) and a high of 40. For most purposes, five to ten experts represent a sufficiently large group. Using fewer than five experts runs a serious risk of having an unacceptably low level of inter-rater reliability, and using more than 10, although desirable (after all, the more experts, the higher the inter-rater reliability is likely to be), is rarely necessary and can become expensive and burdensome (see LIMITATIONS section).

VALIDITY

A central issue regarding the validity of any test is whether the test is measuring what it's supposed to measure, and one of the strengths of the CAT is its strong face validity; typically, it measures exactly what it looks like it measures. The CAT assesses the creativity of a variety of products (the poems, collages, or other artifacts) created by subjects in the same way that creativity is assessed at the genius level—by experts in that field. And although it is true that experts don't always agree and expert opinion may change over time, at a given point in time there is no more objective or valid measure of the creativity of a work of art than the collective judgments of artists and art critics, just as there is no more valid measure of the creativity of a scientific theory than the collective opinions of scientists working in that field. And for more the everyday, garden-variety creativity of most creativity research, the fact that fields may experience paradigm shifts over time will have little practical significance because few if any subjects in such studies are doing creative work that is at the cutting edge of a domain. The high inter-rater reliability evidence previously cited attest to the fact that experts *do* tend to agree on which artifacts are highly creative and which are not. Certainly, however, there are cases in which experts can agree and still be wrong (for many years, most experts agreed that it was not necessary for a doctor to wash her or his hands before operating on a patient!).

CAT creativity ratings have been shown to be assessments of *creativity*, not of unrelated attributes of the artifacts being judged. For example, working with the artistic creativity task of collage-making, Amabile (1982, 1983) demonstrated not only that experts tend to agree in their judgments of creativity, but also that these creativity ratings were not the same as judgments of such attributes as technical goodness (r with creativity ratings = .13), neatness (r with creativity ratings = $-.26$), or expression (r with creativity ratings = $-.05$). She did find strong positive correlations with many other judgments, such as novel use of materials (r with creativity ratings = .81), complexity (r with creativity ratings = .76), and aesthetic appeal (r with creativity ratings = .43), but most people would agree that all of these aspects of a collage should be related to the creativity of that collage. A factor analysis of 23 different ratings produced two factors, creativity and technical goodness. A similar study using poetry writing as the task produced similar results, with three factors emerging: creativity, style, and technical correctness.

CAT ratings of poems, stories, and collages have been shown to be associated with convincing evidence of validity in the assessment of poetry-writing, story-writing, and collage-making creativity. It is less clear whether these measures also assess more general creativity-relevant abilities, a topic about which there has been much debate (see, e.g.., Amabile, 1983, 1996; Baer, 1993, 1994a, 1996, 1998a; Conti, Coon, & Amabile, 1996; Plucker, 1998; Plucker & Runco, 1998; Runco, 1987). If creativity varies by domain, as many have argued, then the notion of a single creativity score simply makes no sense. On the other hand, to the extent that creativity is thought to be a general trait or set of skills that can be applied in any field (so that the same creativity-relevant skills could help one be a more creative poet, a more creative scientist, or a more creative chef), a single creativity score is a coherent construct. CAT assessments of creativity generally show little domain generality (that is, correlations of ratings of subjects' creativity in different domains tend to hover near zero, especially if variance attributable to general intelligence is removed; Baer, 1993, 1994a, 1998a). Other kinds of creativity measures, such as divergent-thinking test scores, creative activity checklists, or personality checklists, all of which tend to assume that creativity is more domain-general, have been shown to exhibit greater domain generality than the CAT (Kaufman, Cole, & Baer, in press; Plucker, 1998; Plucker, & Runco, 1998).

CAT assessments of creativity are normative within the group of artifacts being judged, but these ratings cannot yield standardized scores of any kind; as noted in the previous paragraph, CAT scores are also not good measures of overall creativity. Despite these limitations, the CAT is a technique that can be used by many different researchers. For example, it can be used equally well by researchers who believe that creativity has a significant domain-transcending, general component (e.g.,

Amabile, 1983, 1996), those who argue for a highly domain-specific understanding of creativity (e.g., Baer, 1994a, 1996), or even those who may be trying to separate domain-general and domain-specific variance in creativity (e.g., Baer, 1993; Conti, Coon, & Amabile, 1996). This would be impossible with most creativity tests (such as the widely used divergent-thinking tests) because such tests *assume* a high level of generality of creativity.

It is more difficult to discuss questions of predictive validity because of the inherent limitations of the CAT. A high CAT score in poetry writing would predict writing creative poetry – but nothing else. Comparisons between consensual assessment and more traditional psychometric techniques (Amabile, Phillips, & Collins, 1994; Runco, 1989a) have yet to produce definitive conclusions.[2] Runco, McCarthy, and Svenson (1994) and Amabile (1996) and her colleagues report moderate relationships between self-ratings and expert ratings of products. In general, individuals give themselves a higher evaluation than do judges, which may not be terribly surprising to those (such as the first author) who have taken many classes in creative writing. Despite a difference in magnitude, self-ratings and expert-rated work shows similar rank ordering of products and moderate correlations.

However, CAT ratings are generally quite stable across time (Baer, 1994b), indicating that earlier CAT scores do predict later CAT scores. It would also be feasible to investigate the question historiometrically (does past creative work predict later creative work), and an initial study of Mozart's life indicates that the answer is yes (Kozbelt, 2005). However, CAT scores would not be expected to predict other notable outcomes. Despite the stability of CAT ratings, they nonetheless respond well to real within-subject changes in motivation (e.g., Amabile, 1996; Baer, 1997, 1998b) or increases in skill based on training (e.g., Baer,

---

2. One counterargument could be that expert-evaluated creativity is the criterion against which other measures are evaluated (Baer, 1993a).

========

≡ Rapid Reference 3.2

Reliability and Validity of the CAT

- Acceptable evidence of inter-rater reliability (typically .70–.90) among experts
- Reliability assessed with Cronbach's coefficient alpha, the Spearman-Brown prediction formula, or the intraclass correlation method
- Strong evidence of construct validity as an assessment of creativity in a particular domain
- Not a measure of general (overall) creativity

========

1994a). This has enabled the CAT to be used to assess the impact of varying constraints on creative performance (see Rapid Reference 3.2).

COMMON TASKS USED IN THE CAT

The most extensively used and validated CAT tasks are collage making, poetry writing, story writing, and storytelling.

In collage making, subjects are given a set of pre-cut construction paper shapes and asked to make a collage. Here is how one researcher described the task: In the collage-making task, subjects were given a blank 14" × 22" piece of white tagboard, a bottle of glue, and a set of over one hundred pre-cut construction paper designs (including hearts, butterflies, squares, circles, and triangles of various colors) and asked to make an "interesting, silly design." The materials each student received were identical. There was no time limit, but most students finished in less than 20 minutes. The collages were later rated for creativity by art educators. (Baer, 1993, pp. 60–61)

In the poetry-writing task, subjects are given a topic, and sometimes a poetic form, and asked to write a poem. For example, these are the set of instructions given to one set of subjects: On the next page, you are asked to write a poem using the format called SciFaiku. SciFaiku is a form of poetry derived from haiku, a traditional Japanese poetry form composed of three lines of less than 17 syllables. The topic is science fiction. It strives for a directness of expression and beauty in its simplicity. SciFaiku also frequently strives for insightful commentary on the human condition. Here is an example:

on blackhole's edge
indecision
drifts me in

- You can also write more than one stanza, following the same rule of three lines of each. Here is another example:

Hydroponics bay
a snail among stars
on the wide porthole glass.
Mid-spring, anticipating
the imminent cloning
of humans.
Bathing
her reptilian skin—
small bubbles on glossy green.

- In the space provided below, please write a SciFaiku poem, with a theme of science fiction. You can write anything you like, as far as your poem follows the rule of haiku (three lines of less than 17 syllables in one stanza). You should spend about 10 minutes on this, but please take your time. (Kaufman et al., in press)

These poems were later rated by experts, all of whom worked independently of one another and with no knowledge of who wrote the poems. Here are the instructions the experts received:

- Please read through these poems twice. The first time, assign a Low, Medium, or High rating. The second time, assign a numerical rating between 1 to 6, with 1 being the least creative and 6 being the most creative. There should be a roughly even number of poems at each of the six levels, but the numbers needn't be *exactly* the same. It is very important that you use the full 1-6 scale, however, and not assign almost all poems the same rating.

  There is no need to explain or defend your ratings in any way; we ask only that you use your expert sense of which are more or less creative. Simply write the number on the paper (1, 2, 3, 4, 5, or 6—or, if you would find it helpful, any decimal from 1.00 to 6.00—but nothing below 1.00 or above 6.00 please; Kaufman et al., in press)

In the storytelling task, subjects are given a story title, or in some cases a prompt such as a drawing, and asked to write a story. Here is one such set of instructions, followed by the directions the expert judges received:

- (Instructions to subjects) In the story-writing test, students were given a line drawing of a girl and a boy dancing or jumping near what might be interpreted as the remains of a picnic lunch. They were asked to write an original story in which the boy and the girl played some part.
- (Instructions to expert judges) There is only one criterion in rating these tests: creativity. I realize that creativity doesn't exist in a vacuum, and to some extent creativity probably overlaps other criteria one might apply—aesthetic appeal, organization, richness of imagery, sophistication of expression, novelty of word choice, appropriateness of word choice, and possibly even correctness of grammar, for example— but I ask you to rank the stories solely on the basis of your thoughtful-but-subjective opinions of their creativity. The point is, you are the expert, and you needn't defend your

choices or articulate a definition of creativity. What creativity means to you can remain a mystery—what I want you to do is use that mysterious expert sense to rank order the stories for creativity. (Baer, 1993)

The storytelling task is a variant on the story-writing task used primarily with very young subjects who may have difficulty writing a story. Subjects are given a picture book and asked to tell a story to go with the pictures. Here is how one researcher described how this task was presented to subjects:

- In the story-telling test, subjects were shown a picture book (A Boy, a Dog, a Frog, and a Friend; Mayer & Mayer, 1971). After looking through it to become familiar with the story, they were instructed to "tell the story in your own words by saying one thing about each page" while looking at the book's pictures. These stories were later transcribed and given to experts to rate for creativity. (Baer, 1993, p. 61)

The instructions given to the raters were essentially the same as those given in the story-writing task.

The CAT has also been used to judge the creativity of such diverse tasks as dramatic performance (Myford, 1989), musical compositions (Hickey, 2001), mathematical equations created by children and adolescents (Baer, 1993), captions written to pictures (Sternberg & Lubart, 1995), personal narratives (Baer, Kaufman, & Gentile, 2002), and mathematical word problems (Baer, 1993).

APPLICATIONS

The CAT is widely used in creativity research. CAT ratings can also be used within classrooms to assess creativity, such as for admission to special programs that specifically look for people who excel in an area of creativity (such as poetry, art, or inventing). CAT ratings can be used to compare one student's creativity on a particular task to the creativity of other students on that same task, but creativity may vary a great deal from domain to domain (and even on tasks in the same general area; see Baer, 1993). Because of this limitation, CAT ratings are not the best way to compare students' creativity more generally. As noted above, it is also not possible to devise any meaningful norms for use in comparing ratings on different CAT-based assessments, and therefore the primary use of the CAT has been in creativity research, not in classroom applications.

The CAT has been widely used in studies that compare subjects' creativity under different conditions. Amabile (1983) originally developed the CAT in order to conduct a wide range of studies looking at the impact on creative performance of manipulating motivational constraints, and she and others have reported several scores of studies comparing creative performance under differing conditions of intrinsic and extrinsic motivation. Others have used the CAT in a wide variety of ways, such as:

- to look at the effects on creativity of teaching different skills and content knowledge (e.g., Baer, 1993, 1997, 2003);
- to test the degree to which creativity is either a general or a domain-specific skill (e.g., Baer, 1993; Conti, Coon, & Amabile, 1996; Runco, 1987; Ruscio, Whitney, & Amabile, 1998);
- to study possible gender and ethnicity differences in creativity (e.g., Kaufman, Baer, & Gentile, 2004);
- to study the relationship between process and product in creativity (e.g., Hennessey, 1994);
- to compare ways in which motivational constraints impact boys and girls differently (e.g., Baer, 1997, 1998b);
- to study creativity in cross-cultural settings (e.g., Niu, in press; Niu & Sternberg, 2001);

- to investigate the long-term stability of creative performance in a given domain (e.g., Baer, 1994a);
- to examine ways that people with different levels of expertise might understand creativity differently (e.g., Kaufman et al, in press; Kaufman, Gentile, & Baer, 2005).

Although the CAT is most often used to judge the creativity of artifacts that have been created under identical conditions (e.g., with the same prompt and instructions given to all subjects, and with the same time limitations), it has recently been demonstrated that the CAT also works effectively and reliably when the artifacts whose creativity is to be judged (such as poems or stories) have been created under somewhat different conditions (Baer, Kaufman, & Gentile, 2004). This allows the use of the CAT not only in tightly controlled experimental studies, but also in research that employs creative products that have been created for other purposes. For example, the CAT could be used to compare the effectiveness of different prompts or instructions given to students. Some such prompts or instructions could be shown to result in more creative products (stories, essays, etc.) based on the creativity ratings of the experts. The artifacts still must be of the same kind, however (e.g., all poems, or all collages, or all stories). You cannot mix different kinds of artifacts and have expert judges produce meaningful comparative ratings of creativity. (To do so would be rather like asking which is more fruity, apples or oranges.)

In schools, the CAT can be used to judge student creativity in a particular area (or several areas) for such purposes as admission to a program for gifted and talented students. If the program focuses on a particular domain—for example, a magnet school for students gifted in science, or in the visual arts, or in some other area—then the appropriate tasks would naturally be drawn from those domains. If the goal is to find students who are highly creative for a program that does not specialize in one domain, but instead is interested in assessing student creativity more generally, two approaches are possible. In both cases one needs to assess creativity on a variety of tasks from different domains—perhaps a collage-making task, a poetry-writing task, and a design-an-experiment (science) task—each of which would be judged by experts in that particular domain. One could then either select students who showed the greatest creativity on any one of the tasks or sum the scores for a more general creativity index.

LIMITATIONS

The CAT can be used only for within-group comparisons, and is therefore not appropriate for individual testing (unless a group of subjects will all be tested individually and comparisons made of creativity ratings within the group). There are no standardized scores (or scoring techniques), and subjects in two different samples that were judged separately cannot be compared. The CAT can only be used when comparisons within a particular group of subjects are needed (and all artifacts must have been judged by the same panel of experts).

The CAT is also very resource-intensive: Subjects must actually create the artifacts to be judged (poems, collages, stories, etc.), and then panels of expert judges must work independently to judge the creativity of those artifacts. The CAT thus requires more time (and especially the time of expert judges) than most other methods of creativity assessment. Expert judges are often difficult to find, usually need to be paid money, and may develop rater fatigue after a certain number of ratings.

The general question of who is a good expert or not represents another challenge when doing research using the CAT. Runco and Chand (1994), for example, suggest that experts who can judge their own products effectively do not necessarily possess the ability to evaluate the creative products of other individuals.

Some domains lend themselves more to finding appropriate judges than do others. In a very specific domain, such as writing haikus, there are some obvious choices for experts (master haiku writers, poetry professors who teach haiku, etc.). Yet how far along the continuum can one go? Are graduate students in poetry acceptable raters? How about people who like haikus? People who have written haikus for fun (but perhaps not good ones)? It is a slippery slope. There is some evidence that some leeway can be given; Baer, Kaufman, and Gentile (2004) used 13 experts to rate creative stories, poems, and narratives. Their judges were psychologists who study creativity, creative writers, and teachers who had taught creative writing. Generally, all three groups showed strong reliability, and all three groups' opinions were significantly correlated. In an extension, Kaufman, Gentile, and Baer (2005) had the same creative work rated by gifted novices (high school students who were selected by the New Jersey Governor's School of the Arts as being gifted and talented in creative writing). These novices also showed high reliability and their ratings significantly correlated with the ratings of all three expert groups (the relationship with the writers' ratings, not surprisingly, was the highest).

However, it is possible to go too far down the slope. Some researchers have recently attempted to replace expert raters with non-expert or peer raters. This adjustment is probably motivated by the difficulty and expense of assembling panels of expert judges, but this substitution of novice or peer raters for expert raters is problematic and should probably be avoided for two reasons:

- In terms of the construct validity of the CAT, one cannot claim that non-expert judgments of creativity share the kind of real-world validity that the CAT claims.
- On a more practical note, research suggests that experts and novice raters do not tend to agree closely enough in their ratings to trust novice raters (Kaufman et al., in press), although it is possible that future research may

show that in at least some domains novices can satisfactorily mimic the ratings of experts.

Of course, if one could show that ratings of creativity on a particular task with a particular use of novice raters would yield essentially the same ratings as ratings by appropriate experts, there is no reason why such a substitution would not be permissible. Dollinger and Shafran (2005) have done just that on one rather specialized task—rating the creativity of drawings produced using the Test of Creative Thinking-Drawing Production. The procedure used a brief training procedure to help the novices match their ratings with those of experts. In this case, however, experts are still required to make judgments on the pool of drawings to be rated, ratings that can then be used to train the novices, and it therefore does not eliminate the need for expert raters.

Although the CAT uses ratings from experts who do not communicate with each other, other expert ratings that do allow such communication would be vulnerable to several possible influences and biases, such as groupthink and functional fixedness. In addition, most studies using the CAT are centered on a few core domains (creative writing, art, mathematical equations, and music composition). There is not adequate evidence to assume that this methodology would work equally well across every domain, or that the same level of expert would be needed. An expert rating creativity in medicine, for example, may need a much higher level of domain-specific knowledge that an expert rating finger-painting.

HOW TO USE THE CAT

Choosing an appropriate task

The first thing one must do when using the CAT is to determine the domain of creativity one wishes to assess. Choosing an appropriate task is crucial. If one is interested in subjects' artistic creativity, asking them to write poems and having judges evaluate the creativity of those poems makes little sense. The task in that case would need to be one that involved artistic expression, such as the collage-making task described previously.

Here are some examples of ways to choose CAT tasks for particular purposes.

If you are interested in subjects' creativity in a particular domain, then obviously the task should be from that domain. But what kind of task? Things to consider include the time it will take subjects to create the artifacts, the materials they will need, and special skills that might be required to do the task. For example, if the domain in question is artistic creativity, asking subjects to create a sculpture might be problematic in many ways: It might take a great deal of time; it would require significant special materials; and it would also require skill in one particular sub-domain of artistic creativity (sculpture). Unless you are specifically interested in creativity in sculpting, it would therefore probably be a poor choice. Other kinds of art might require few specialized materials—sketching, for instance—but these require levels of skill that it might not be appropriate to assume your subjects will have. For example, asking subjects to create a sketch of some kind might inappropriately advantage students with training in sketching. If all students have had such training (or would be expected to have the relevant skills), then this would work fine. But there are also art-related tasks that require no special skills (and that would therefore not advantage some subjects over others). The collage-making activity that Amabile invented (1982, 1983) has been used widely for precisely this reason.

If you are interested in creativity of a specific kind, then the choice is relatively easy. For example, Baer (1996) wanted to test whether divergent-thinking training related to one task would enhance creativity on other tasks within the same domain. He trained experimental group subjects in divergent-thinking skills hypothesized to increase poetry-writing creativity, while the control group received unrelated training. He then had subjects write both poems and short stories. Both poems and stories were later judged by appropriate panels of judges for creativity. (He found that the training did increase poetry-writing creativity, but did not increase short story-writing creativity.)

If you really don't care about the domain, then the choice of task is especially easy. You want a task that anyone can do at some level and that will not favor any group of subjects inappropriately. For example, when Amabile (1983) wanted to see if expecting that one's work will be evaluated impacted creativity, she wanted tasks that required no special training or skills. In some of these studies she used collage making, in others poetry writing. (Anticipating evaluation led to lower creativity in both cases.) In cases like these there is special value in using tasks that have been used before and are well-validated, such as collage making, poetry writing, story writing, or storytelling, as described previously.

In some cases you may be using previously created artifacts (e.g., projects completed for some other purpose, such as stories or other writings students have collected in portfolios). Although the artifacts need not be exactly parallel—they might, for example, be stories written in response to different prompts—they need to be at least similar in the ways they were collected (see the next section for guidance regarding the collection of artifacts) and of the same kind (i.e., all must be either stories *or* poems; you can't include some stories and some poems in the same group of artifacts to be judged).

Four sets of instructions for different tasks can be found in the previous section, COMMON TASKS USED IN THE CAT.

Collecting the Artifacts

Subjects can work individually or in groups on the task as long as they cannot readily observe the ways others are approaching the task. It is important that the conditions be the same (or as identical as possible).

One such condition that should be the same for all subjects is time constraints. Subjects should have sufficient time to complete the task—the CAT is not a speeded test—and ideally there should be no time limit, but having a time limit is not a problem as long as the time limit allows almost all subjects adequate time to complete the task.

Another standardization procedure is to make sure that all students receive the same (or very similar) instructions (except in the special case where the goal is to compare the impact of giving different sets of instructions to different groups of subjects). If subjects are told the purpose of the task, or if they are told that they should try to be creative, then all subjects should receive the same information (again, the one exception to this is when the goal is to determine the impact of different instructions). In general subjects will assume that the collages, poems, stories, and so on will be evaluated, and it is especially important that all subjects receive similar direction (or, in the case perhaps of a research study, misdirection), because Amabile (1996) has shown that the expectation of evaluation greatly influences creative performance. The same is true of rewards: If subjects are to be rewarded for participation, all subjects need to be rewarded in the same way. Both rewards and the expectation that one's work will be evaluated have been shown to be particularly detrimental to girls' creativity (Baer, 1997, 1998b).

Assembling a Panel of Experts

One of the more challenging (and often time-consuming) jobs you must undertake when using the CAT is finding appropriate experts to judge the artifacts that your subjects will create. Here are some guidelines.

Different artifacts require different kinds of expertise. Experts must know the domain in which they are being asked to make judgments, of course, but judges of student writing do not need the same level of expertise as Pulitzer Prize committees. Research is currently underway to help determine appropriate levels of expertise for different creativity-judging tasks, but a good general set of guidelines would include:

- Judges should have a level of expertise that is clearly higher than the presumed level of expertise of the subjects creating the artifacts.
- Judges should have some familiarity with the population from which the subjects are drawn. For example, judges of middle school student work should have some familiarity with middle school student productions in the domain in question. (A Nobel Prize-winning physicist might not be as appropriate as a CAT judge of the creativity of middle school science fair projects as a college science professor who has worked with middle school students in the past.)
- There is no exact number of experts required, but with a very small number it is harder to get good inter-rater reliability coefficients. For most purposes 5–10 judges is an adequate number.

Organizing the Work of the Expert Judges

All judges should receive identical directions, and they should not know the identity of the subjects or anything else about them as individuals (including different conditions under which subjects worked, if there are such differences). It is certainly appropriate that they know the average age of the subjects as a whole, but not their individual ages, as this information might bias their judgments.

Two examples of instructions to judges can be found in the Common Tasks Used in the CAT section. If possible it is best for judges to judge the items in different orders to avoid any influence of the order of judging the artifacts. In most cases judges will work alone, but in some cases they may need to work together in the same room, such as in the judging of collages, which might need to be displayed in such a large area that multiple judging sessions would be difficult to coordinate. In such cases they should be instructed not to discuss or share their ratings in any way until all judgments are complete. (See Rapid Reference 3.3.)

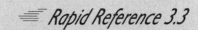

Rapid Reference 3.3

Steps in Using the CAT

- Choose an appropriate task
- Collect the artifacts
- Assemble a panel of experts
- Analyze the results

HOW DO CAT SCORES RELATE TO OTHER MEASURES?

Because the CAT does not yield standardized scores of any kind, little effort has been made to relate creativity ratings based on CAT ratings with other measures, such as intelligence, achievement, personality, or even other measures of creativity ability. Baer (1993a), however, did make several such comparisons. The subjects were all eighth-grade students whose mean verbal and mathematical I.Q. (Differential Abilities Test) and reading and mathematical achievement (California Achievement Test) test scores were well above average. These students produced four separate artifacts:

- *Poetry-writing test:* Subjects were asked to write an original poem on the topic of the four seasons. The form, style, and length of the poem were not specified. Subjects were told that, except for the topic, everything else about the poem was up to them.
- *Story-writing test:* Subjects were given a drawing depicting two men, one neatly and one casually dressed, approaching the corner of a building from opposite directions. They were asked to write an original story in which the two men played some part.

- *Word problem-creating test:* Subjects were asked to write an interesting and original math word problem. They were not asked to solve the problem, but instructed to make sure all needed information was included so that the problem could be solved by someone else.
- *Equation-creating test:* Subjects were given examples of a few equalities (e.g., 2 + 2 = 2 + 2; [9/3][2/6] = [2/3][9/6]) and asked to write an interesting, original equation. (Baer, 1993a, p, 50)

The correlation matrix is reproduced in Table 3.1.

Creative performance on these scales was correlated with both IQ and achievement test scores in the domains in question. Poetry- and story-writing creativity were significantly correlated with verbal IQ and reading achievement scores, and equation-creating creativity was correlated with math IQ and math achievement scores. Creating interesting word problems, which taps skills from both verbal and math domains, was positively correlated with all four IQ and achievement test scores. Because CAT creativity ratings require actual creative performance on real-world tasks—CAT assessments focus on creative products, not creative processes, and do not attempt to tap underlying cognitive abilities—it is no surprise that they are related to both intelligence and achievement, primarily in the general areas most closely related to the activity.

One other finding about CAT creativity ratings is illustrated by the results reported in Table 3.1. First, the CAT ratings on one task, such as story writing, exhibit very small and mostly statistically insignificant correlations with ratings on other tasks. In fact, if variance attributable to IQ and achievement test scores is removed, there is even less correlation across domains, as shown in Table 3.2. CAT-based testing is the most common evidence given of domain-specificity in creativity, whereas other kinds of testing often show greater domain-generality.

Table 3.1. Correlations of CAT and Standardized Test Scores

Test	Poetry	Story	Word Problem	Equation	Verbal IQ	Reading Achieve	Math I.Q.	Math Achieve
Poetry	1.00	.23	.31*	–.14	.44**	.39**	.16	.18
Story		1.00	.20	–.03	.45**	.37**	.14	.09
Word Problem			1.00	–.20	.38**	.36**	.51**	.26
Equation				1.00	.00	.04	.27	.28**
Verbal IQ					1.00	.60**	.45**	.48**
Reading Achievement						1.00	.32*	.49**
Math IQ							1.00	.39**
Math Achievement								1.00

Source: Baer, 1993a, p. 53.

*p < .05 **p < .01 (two-tailed tests) (N = 50)

Table 3.2. Partial Correlations of CAT Ratings (Standardized Test Score Variance Removed) (Baer, 1993, p. 54)

Test	Poetry	Story	Word Problem	Equation
Poetry	1.00	–.01	.19	–.14
Story		1.00	.05	.07
Word Problem			1.00	–.45**
Equation				1.00

Source: Baer, 1993a, p. 53.

**p < .01 (two-tailed test) (N = 50)

Indeed, alternative assessments typically tend to produce these types of results, and traditional assessments tend to show the opposite. The results from the single study reported in Tables 3.1 and 3.2 have been replicated many times with very similar results (e.g., Baer, Kaufman, & Gentile, 2004; Kaufman, Lee, Baer, & Lee, 2007).

THE CAT AND GENDER AND ETHNICITY

People of different ethnicities and genders earn different mean scores on many intelligence, aptitude, and achievement tests, and the issue of how and why differences in intelligence and academic abilities may be related to ethnicity and gender is frequently (and sometimes fiercely) debated (see, e.g., Gallagher & Kaufman, 2005; Gould, 1981; Halpern, 2000; Herrnstein & Murray, 1994; Jacoby & Glauberman, 1995; Pinker & Spelke, 2005).

CAT scores also show little evidence of differences based on ethnicity, at least when differences in IQ scores have been controlled. In one large study, Kaufman, Baer, and Gentile (2004) conducted three separate analyses in which 13 experts rated 103 poems, 104 fictional stories, and 103 personal narratives written by Caucasian, African American, Hispanic American, and Asian American eighth-grade students as a part of the National Assessment of Educational Progress. There were no significant African American-Caucasian differences on any of the writing tasks and there were no gender differences on all three tasks. The only significant differences in the creativity ratings on any of the tasks occurred in poetry, where there were statistically significant differences between the Hispanic American-Caucasian groups and Hispanic American-Asian American groups.

Artwork produced by American college students was rated as more creative than art produced by Chinese students by both American and Chinese raters (Niu & Sternberg, 2001). Yet a similar study that compared American and Chinese drawings of geometric shapes found that the two groups were rated similarly for creativity by both American and Chinese raters (Chen, Kasof, Himsel, Greenberger, Dong, & Gui, 2002). In both studies, American and Chinese judges tended to agree on which products were creative and which products were not creative, although Niu and Sternberg (2001) found that the Chinese judges tended to give higher scores than their American counterparts. There were no differences in rated artwork between Chinese and British schoolchildren, except for the higher ratings earned by Chinese children who attended a weekend art school (Cox, Perara, & Fan, 1998). Another study found Japanese children produced higher rated drawings than British children (Cox, Koyasu, Hiranuma, & Perara, 2001).

Rostan, Pariser, and Gruber (2002) studied Chinese American and European American students' artwork, with two groups in each culture: students with additional art training and classes and students with no such classes. Each group's artwork (one drawing from life and one drawing from imagination) was judged by both Chinese and American judges. There were no significant differences between cultures from either set of judges, only between art students versus non-art students.

Another caveat is that there may be issues of unconscious rater bias in the CAT. Kaufman, Niu, Sexton, and Cole (under review) examined stories and poems written by 205 students and rated by 108 different students. Although there were no significant differences by ethnicity across all raters, it was notable that both European Americans and African Americans preferred stories written by European Americans. A similar study that looked at perceptions and ratings (but did not use the CAT) is Masten, Plata, Wenglar, and Thedford (1999), who found that teachers rated European American students as being more creative than Hispanic American students, with highly acculturated Hispanic Americans receiving higher marks than less acculturated Hispanic Americans.

Although gender differences in creativity test scores have occasionally been reported, overall most creativity testing has produced remarkably little evidence of gender differences (Baer, 2005; Baer, & Kaufman, 2005). This is true of the CAT as well, although as will be explained below, there are two notable caveats to this generalization. Among studies that found little or no gender difference, Amabile (1983) found no significant gender differences in a series of studies of creativity in art using a collage-making task. Using the same task with adults, in one study, "there was a nearly significant sex difference. Females made collages that were rated higher in creativity than those made by males ($p < .052$)" (p. 49), but in other research using the same task there were no significant gender differences. In three studies of verbal creativity among adults using a poetry-writing task, Amabile (1983) reported that there were no significant gender differences. In three additional studies of verbal creativity involving either storytelling by children or caption writing by adults, no gender differences were reported.

In an investigation by Baer (1993a), 50 academically gifted eighth-grade students wrote poems, stories, mathematical word problems, and original mathematical equations. Only among the equations was there a significant gender difference (in which males scored higher than females).

In the six other studies reported, which involved second-, fourth-, and fifth-grade students, as well as one study that focused on adults, no gender differences were observed. In the Kaufman et al. (2004) study mentioned earlier, there were no gender differences either.

The first exception, mentioned above, has to do with the environments in which subjects are working. Amabile (1996) has shown that extrinsic constraints (e.g., rewards or anticipated evaluations) tend to lower creativity scores on the CAT. But with middle school and older students, this effect is primarily evident among girls, not boys. In five studies in which middle school students were asked to make collages, write stories, and/or write poems (Baer, 1997, 1998b), for example, girls generally produced collages, stories, and poems that were judged (using the CAT) to be as creative (or, in some cases, to be more creative than, but in no cases less creative) as those produced by boys when no mention was made of rewards or evaluation. When either rewards or evaluation were made salient, however, the creativity ratings of the girls' collages, stories, and poems plummeted, but there was little difference in the creativity of the boys' collages, stories, and poems. The result was that when (and only when) extrinsic constraints were made highly salient, boys' creative performance was significantly higher than girls' performance.

The second exception centers on a study of trends in the creativity literature. Feist and Runco (1993) counted the numbers of male and female contributors to the *Journal of Creative Behavior* from 1967 until 1989. Over this 22-year period, there were approximately three times as many male authors as female authors (mean number of male authors/article = .93; mean number of female authors/article = .33). The number of female authors increased, however, from a per-issue mean of little more than 0 in 1967 to a per-issue mean of just under 3 for the years 1980–1989. The mean number of male authors per issue dropped during the same period, although only slightly, from about 6 in the late 1960s to about

> **DON'T FORGET**
> ....
> There are few if any differences in creativity ratings related to gender or ethnicity when the Consensual Assessment Technique is used to judge creative products.

5 in the 1980s. The number of women authors reached a plateau in the 1980s. Feist and Runco noted that this follows the trend in other journals, specifically the Australian Journal of Psychology, where the number of women authors increased into the 1970s and then reached a plateau.

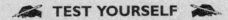

TEST YOURSELF

1. **The Consensual Assessment Technique uses which of the following to assess creativity?**
    (a) Divergent thinking questions
    (b) Actual creative products
    (c) Checklists of interests
    (d) Scoring rubrics

2. **What kind of reliability does the Consensual Assessment Technique claim?**
    (a) Test-retest
    (b) Split-half
    (c) Inter-rater
    (d) Parallel forms
    (e) Internal-consistency

3. **The Consensual Assessment Technique can be used to:**
    (a) compare subjects' overall creativity
    (b) create standardized creativity scores
    (c) compare subjects' creativity in specific domains

4. **The Consensual Assessment Technique is based on which of the following theories of creativity?**

   (a) Structure of the intellect

   (b) Multiple intelligences

   (c) Blind variation and selective retention

   (d) Divergent thinking

   (e) It is not based on any theoretical model

5. **Because the Consensual Assessment Technique has been shown to be reliable, one does not need to test for inter-rater reliability every time the Consensual Assessment Technique is used.** True or False?

6. **Expert judges:**

   (a) are optional

   (b) can be replaced by peer judges

   (c) are required

7. **The artifacts to be judged using the Consensual Assessment Technique:**

   (a) must all be of essentially the same kind (i.e., poems *or* stories, but not poems *and* stories)

   (b) can include a variety of different types of artifacts (i.e., poems, collages, and captions for pictures)

   (c) must include a variety of different types of artifacts (i.e., poems, collages, and captions for pictures)

8. **Creativity ratings using the Consensual Assessment Technique are for the most part NOT related to which of the following?**

   (a) Intelligence test scores

   (b) Ethnicity

   (c) Achievement test scores

Answers: 1. b; 2. c; 3. c; 4. e; 5. False; 6. c; 7. a; 8. b

Four

ASSESSMENT BY OTHERS: TEACHER, PEER, AND PARENT MEASURES

In Chapter One we discussed the "Four P" model of creativity, which distinguishes the creative person, process, product, and press (i.e., environment) (Rhodes, 1961). Assessment of the creativity of individuals by others focuses on the creative *person*. This might include perceptions of personality traits, creativity-relevant abilities, motivation, intelligence, thinking styles, emotional intelligence, or knowledge.

Such an assessment could be as simple as a global rating of an individual's creativity. Teachers, for example, might simply rank order their students based on the teachers' knowledge of the students and the teachers' implicit beliefs about the nature of creativity. This is superficially similar to the Consensual Assessment Technique (CAT) discussed in Chapter Three, which is also a kind of assessment by others. A global assessment of the creativity of one's children, students, employees, fellow students, or coworkers differs from the CAT in several very important ways, however.

The CAT evaluates individual creative products, but the assessments by others that are the focus of this chapter ask raters to judge the creativity of a person as a whole. The emphasis with assessment by others is on the traits and abilities one believes the people being judged possess—traits and abilities one believes are relevant to creativity—and is *not* based on judgments of any particular artifacts they may have created, ideas they may have generated, or work they may have produced.

Global assessments of individual creativity assume that creativity is domain-general. A global assessment of creativity only makes sense if one believes that creativity is a fairly general trait, set of skills, or disposition. Although it is of course possible to rate students' or colleagues' creativity in just one particular area, this is rarely done. Were one to make such a domain-specific rating of students' or colleagues' creativity, however, it is likely that raters would think more about particular creative products (the ideas and creations that individuals have produced) than about personality variables. This kind of assessment would then become more a variant of the CAT than a representative of the kinds of assessment of the creative person that are the focus of this chapter.

The CAT generally requires raters who are experts in the domain of the products to be rated. The people asked to do ratings of the creativity of others, on the other hand, are most often teachers and parents who may have expertise regarding the children being rated but who probably are not experts in creativity. In fact, several studies have suggested that the validity of teachers' ratings of students' creativity is often severely compromised by inadequate conceptions of creativity (Pearlman, 1983; Westby & Dawson, 1995). This is one reason (as we will see below) that assessments of creativity by others do not usually rely on a simple rating or rank ordering, but instead provide guidelines (such as a checklist of traits) developed based on creativity theory and research.

When using the CAT, raters do not know who created whatever artifacts (poems, stories, collages, etc.) being judged for creativity. This prevents anything that the rater may know about the creator and whatever attitudes or feelings the rater may have toward that person from influencing the assessment process. In assessments of creativity by others, however, the assessor must know the person (and the more familiar the rater is with that person the better). This allows personal attitudes (such as halo effects and biases of any kind, both positive and negative) to influence these global assessments of creativity by others.

VALIDITY OF GLOBAL ASSESSMENTS OF CREATIVITY BY OTHERS

There is little in the way of validity data for global assessments of the creativity of others beyond some cautionary research (Pearlman, 1983; Westby & Dawson, 1995) about the use of unguided teacher ratings of creativity. Many personality variables often associated with creativity (e.g., risk-taking behavior, independent thinking, impulsivity, and non-conformity) may not be seen as positive traits by many teachers, who might therefore miscategorize students who exhibit such traits. Similarly, some traits that are negatively associated with creativity but favored by many teachers (e.g., reliability, rule-following behavior, or conformity) might also lead to mislabeling of students because of a halo effect. This is true even when teachers profess to like and favor creative students.

Westby and Dawson (1995) asked college students and elementary teachers to rate a series of 50 descriptions based on how closely they connected the descriptions to creativity in eight-year-old children. They reported the 10 most and 10 least descriptive adjectives or phrases. The ratings of the college students closely tracked those of creativity researchers, yielding a "95% agreement with past research. The only item that diverged from previous work was 'is appreciative'" (p. 4). The 10 descriptors most and least associated with creativity are shown in Table 4.1.

The ratings made by teachers (all elementary school teachers) were quite different, however. The teachers were given just the list of the 20 most and least descriptive adjectives and phrases from the following table. Their ratings are shown in Table 4.2.

> **DON'T FORGET**
> ....
> Assessments of creativity by others are often influenced by the attitudes and beliefs of those doing the ratings. This could compromise the validity of the assessments.

Of the 10 descriptions most closely associated with creativity on the college students' list (which very closely match those of creativity theorists), only four

Table 4.1. Characteristics of a Creative 8-Year-Old Child?
College Student Ratings

Characteristic	M
Most Typical of a Creative Child	
Makes Up the Rules as He or She Goes Along	7.30
Is Impulsive	7.29
Is a Nonconformist	7.29
Is Emotional	7.19
Is Progressive	7.00
Is Determined	6.91
Is Individualistic	6.90
Takes Chances	6.90
Tends Not to Know Own Limitations and Tries to Do What Others Think Is Impossible	6.77
Likes to be Alone When Creating Something New	6.77
Least Typical of a Creative Child	
Is Tolerant	4.52
Is Practical	4.53
Is Reliable	4.77
Is Dependable	4.78
Is Responsible	4.97
Is Logical	5.34
Is Understanding	5.50
Is Appreciative	5.72
Is Good-Natured	6.00
Is Sincere	6.03

Source: Westby & Dawson, 1995, p. 5. Reprinted with permission of author and Taylor and Francis: www.informaworld.com

were included on the teachers' list of highly creative attributes, with the remaining six listed by the teachers as least typical of a creative child. The correlation between the two lists was just $r(18) = .20$. A separate part of this study looked at the characteristics of students that teachers liked most and least. The list of characteristics teachers like most was very similar to their list of behaviors they associated with creativity. It

Table 4.2. Characteristics of a Creative 8-Year-Old Child? Teacher Ratings

Characteristic	M
Most Typical of a Creative Child	
Is Individualistic	8.13
Takes Chances	7.67
Is Progressive	7.53
Is Determined	7.53
Is Sincere	7.00
Is Appreciative	7.00
Is Good-Natured	6.93
Is Responsible	6.87
Is Logical	6.80
Is Reliable	6.80
Least Typical of a Creative Child	
Is Practical	5.53
Makes Up the Rules as He or She Goes Along	5.80
Is Emotional	5.93
Is Understanding	6.07
Is Tolerant	6.20
Is Impulsive	6.20
Is a Nonconformist	6.33
Tends Not to Know Own Limitations and Tries to Do What Others Think Is Impossible	6.53
Likes to Be Alone When Creating Something New	6.60
Is Dependable	6.70

Source: Westby & Dawson, 1995, p. 7. Reprinted with permission of author and Taylor and Francis: www.informaworld.com

was clear that teachers' perceptions of traits associated with creativity were biased in the direction of traits that they found likable.

OVERVIEW OF CREATIVITY CHECKLISTS

There is reason, as explained above, to distrust teacher ratings, and probably parent and supervisor ratings as well if they are based simply on global impressions. To limit this kind of unintended bias, raters are generally given checklists of traits which they are instructed to rate separately for each child. These ratings are then summed to produce an overall creativity rating.

There are many such checklists, mostly designed for use in schools, and we will discuss several commercially available checklists of this kind below. Few, quite frankly, have been able to produce strong validity evidence, which is rather difficult to collect (and even when collected often depends on the presumed validity of other creativity measures, such as tests of divergent thinking, because others kinds of validation studies, while possible, are both time-consuming and expensive). Most of these checklists do have reasonable face validity, which is to say they match fairly well what most researchers and theorists suggest are skills, traits, and dispositions often associated with creativity. How accurately and objectively the respondents are able to assess such skills, traits, and dispositions is hard to determine, but the study reported above suggests we should interpret any such results with a great deal of caution.

Many creativity checklists are sold commercially and copyright protected, but some are freely available. Table 4.3 shows one such Creativity Checklist (Proctor & Burnett, 2004).

This scale employs a three-point Likert scale: 1 = rarely, 2 = sometimes, and 3 = often. A total score can be computed simply by summing rankings. There are no norms for the checklist, and it is perhaps most appropriately used to make comparisons within a group of students, not between students who were part of separate rating groups. Just as (when using the CAT) a poem that in one sample might stand out as very creative but as part of another sample might show only average creativity, a student who might seem to be a very imaginative thinker compared to one group of students might seem less so compared to a different group. The fairly explicit Performance Indicators and the 3-point Likert scale ratings ("rarely," "sometimes," "often") are designed to clarify, in a more criterion-referenced way, what each rating might be intended to mean, but there is sufficient flexibility and need for interpretation that

Table 4.3. The Creativity Checklist Items and Their Performance Indicators

Item/ Descriptor	Performance Indicators
1. A fluent thinker	The student . . . is full of ideas; finds different ways of doing things; answers questions fluently and readily; hypothesizes easily; generally possesses high verbal fluency; can list, tell/retell, label, and compile easily; answers (fluently) questions such as How many? Why? What are the possible reasons for? Just suppose . . . ?
2. A flexible thinker	The student . . . can solve, change, adapt, modify, magnify, rearrange, reverse, and improve; is versatile and can cope with several ideas at once; is constructive and mentally builds and rebuilds; is sensitive to new ideas and flexible in approach to problems; can tolerate ambiguity.
3. An original thinker	The student . . . can create, invent, make up, construct, substitute, combine, compose, improve, and design; is attracted by novelty, complexity, mystery; asks What if? questions.
4. An elaborative thinker	The student . . . can enlarge, extend, exchange, replace, and modify; goes beyond assigned tasks; sees new possibilities in the familiar; embellishes stories/situations.
5. An intrinsically motivated student	The student . . . often seeks out knowledge independently; does a job well for its own sake, not for rewards; appears to enjoy learning for learning's sake.
6. A curious student	The student . . . tries to discover the unusual or find out more about a topic of interest; unable to rest until the work is complete; possesses a sense of wonder and intrigue; possesses a high energy level; is adventurous and engages in spontaneous action; can uncover, investigate, question, research, analyze, seek out, and ponder.

Table 4.3. Continued

Item/Descriptor	Performance Indicators
7. A risk taker	The student . . . will challenge, criticize, judge, question, dispute, and decide; not afraid to try new things; not afraid to fail; can rank and give reasons, justify and defend, contrast and compare, devise a plan, make a choice between.
8. An imaginative or intuitive thinker	The student . . . will fantasize, create, compose, invent, suppose, dramatize, design, dream, wish; is perceptive and sees relationships; can make mental leaps from one idea to another and from the known to the unknown.
9. A student who engages in complex tasks and enjoys a challenge	The student . . . can evaluate, generalize, abstract, reflect upon, move from concrete to abstract, move from general to specific, converge and has problem tolerance; is not easily stressed; does not give up easily; often irritated by the routine and obvious.

Source: Proctor & Burnett, 2004, p. 426.

we think it unlikely that there would not be a significant comparison group effect.

As with most creativity checklists, there is no criterion-related or predictive validity data for Proctor and Burnett's (2004) Creativity Checklist. They did do a factor analysis of scores of elementary school children and found a single factor solution that accounted for 63 percent of variance, and a correlation matrix of all nine descriptors revealed that every one of the descriptors was significantly correlated with every other. It is possible, of course, that because these descriptors all describe traits or abilities associated with creativity, teachers who rated students tended to make, in effect, a global rating of the creativity of each student, which would then influence all their ratings for that student. But this checklist approach at least clarifies for teachers (or other raters) what is meant

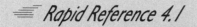

Rapid Reference 4.1

Overview of the Assessments of Creativity by Others

- Generally focuses on global assessments of creativity—the creativity of the person being rated as a whole, not on creativity on a particular task or in a particular domain.
- Raters should know the people being rated well.
- Personal attitudes and beliefs of the raters can bias these global assessments of creativity by others.

by creativity for the purposes of the assessment. (See Rapid Reference 4.1.)

Commercially Available Checklists for Rating Creativity

The Scales for Rating the Behavioral Characteristics of Superior Students (SRBCSS; Renzulli et al., 2004) is an instrument that is widely used in the selection of students for gifted and talented programs (Callahan et al., 1995; Hunsaker & Callahan, 1995). The SRBCSS was among the first scales designed to introduce teacher perspectives into the gifted identification process (Bracken & Brown, 2006). It is based on a multiple talent approach to the identification of gifted students (Renzulli, 1986; see Chapter Six) and includes 14 scales to help identify student abilities in the following areas:

- learning
- motivation
- creativity
- leadership
- art
- music
- dramatics
- planning

- communication (precision)
- communication (expression)
- mathematics
- reading
- science
- technology

The creativity scale was based on a literature review and feedback from educators. The publisher reports no criterion-related validity information, but reliability is good if those completing the assessment (usually teachers) have been trained (Center for Creative Learning, 2002b). A study on the validity of an earlier version of the scales concluded that the SRBCSS scales were correlated to a low degree with the traditional cognitive tests but highly interrelated among themselves. Subsequent factor analysis yielded two factors, with the SRBCSS loading on a single Teacher Judgment Factor and the other measures loading on a Scholastic Aptitude Factor.

Interpretation of the results suggest that the validity of the SRBCSS subscales for measuring separate sets of characteristics is questionable. However, the scales appear to make teacher ratings more objective (Gridley & Treloar, 1984, p. 65). The loading on a "single Teacher Judgment Factor" suggests, as discussed previously, the probability that the teachers who did the ratings may have tended to make an implicit global rating of the talents of each student, which then influenced all their ratings for that student.

Reviews of the first edition of the SRBCSS were generally positive, praising the ease of administration and clear guidelines for teachers (Argulewicz, 1985; Rust, 1985).

Information about the rating scales, including sample items and training materials, is available at http://www.creativelearningpress .com/clp/662.html.

The Williams Scale of the Creativity Assessment Packet

The Williams Scale (Williams, 1980) is a checklist that is part of a larger assessment package that is widely used in selection of students for gifted and talented programs. The website for the Creativity Assessment Packet states that:

> The Creativity Assessment Packet (CAP) measures the cognitive thought factors of fluency, flexibility, elaboration, originality, vocabulary, and comprehension. CAP is a test packet consisting of two group-administered instruments for children: the Test of Divergent Thinking (Forms A and B) and the Test of Divergent Feeling. A third instrument, The Williams Scale, is a rating instrument for teachers and parents of the same tested factors among children. All three instruments can be used to evaluate, screen, and identify the most important factors of creativity found in some degree among all children. CAP is suitable for children ages 6 through 18 and is self-scoring (from the ProEd website: http://www.proedinc.com/customer/product View.aspx?ID=777).

The 48 items of the Williams Scale can be completed by a teacher, caregiver, or parent in 10–20 minutes. Table 4.4 lists the eight item types and a sample charac-teristic. For all questions, the teacher or parent places either a double check (✓✓) when the characteristic is present most of the time; a single check (✓) when the characteristic is present occasionally; or leaves the item blank if the characteristic is rarely or never present.

The publisher does not provide either validity or reliability information. In a review of the CAP, Cooper (1991) wrote that the Williams Scale, and teacher or parent creativity rating scales more generally, "are many times misunderstood and misused in their actual administration" (p. 196). They conclude that the Williams Scale "could not be recom-

Table 4.4. Examples of Items on the Williams Scales

Observational Topic	Sample characteristic
Fluent	The student who usually has several ideas about something instead of one.
Flexible	The student who shifts and can take another point of view or considers situations differently from others.
Original	The student who enjoys the unusual and dislikes doing things the way everyone else does them.
Elaborate	The student who will want to "jazz up" or embellish upon the work or ideas of others.
Curious/Inquisitive	The student who continually explores books, games, maps, pictures, etc.
Imaginative (Visualize/Dream)	The student who can see things in a picture or drawing that no one else has seen.
Complex	The student who thrives in trying again and again in order to gain success.
Courageous/Risk Taker	The student who is not concerned by disapproval from classmates, teachers, or parents.

Source: Adapted from http://www.hpedsb.on.ca/ec/services/spe/documents/williams_scale.pdf.

mended as an adequate assessment of the complex dimensions of creativity" (p. 196). Both Rosen (1985) and Damarin (1985), in reviewing the Williams Scale as part of the larger CAP, criticize poor technical qualities and question its usefulness in general. In addition, the Center for Creative Learning (2002a) rates both the validity and reliability of the Williams Scale to be poor. However, Cameron, Meyer, Brown, Carson, and Bittner (1993) found that both the fluency and imagination observational topics were positively and significantly correlated with color discrimination.

Ideal Child Checklist

Torrance's (1975; Torrance & Sisk, 1997) Ideal Child Checklist is not a measure of individual creativity, but is used instead as a measure of attitudes toward creativity. For example, Reffel (2003) used the Ideal Child Checklist in a study that showed creative teachers had more favorable attitudes toward creative students than did less creative teachers. The Ideal Child Checklist includes creativity as one thing being assessed among others. It "was developed to provide a criterion of the productive, creative person . . . [and] has been used extensively in studies involving perceptions of parents, teachers, and children of the ideal pupil" (Paguio, 1983, p. 571).

A factor analysis of the Ideal Child Checklist revealed four factors. According to this analysis, the ideal child is:

- confident, aggressive, and well-adjusted
- sociable
- not stubborn, domineering, haughty, fearful, fault-finding, or trouble-making
- creative and intuitive

Only the last of the four factors (creative and intuitive) relates clearly to creativity, and this factor had the weakest reliability of the four (Paguio, 1983). The Ideal Child Checklist may, therefore, be an appropriate measure of parent, teacher, or student values, but caution should be exercised in using it (or any measure that includes creativity as just one subsumed dimension in an assessment with some other goal) as an indicator of creativity or (as in this case) attitudes toward creativity.

Other Rating Scales

Several other rating scales have been produced and initially studied; none of these measures, however, have been adequately studied for validity and reliability, nor are the measures regularly used in the creativity literature. For example, the Gifted Evaluation Scale-Second Edition (Henage, McCarney & Anderson, 1998; GES-2) consists of 48 items designed to rate students' abilities in the following areas:

- Intellectual
- Creativity
- Specific Academic Aptitude
- Leadership Ability
- Performing and Visual Arts

The original GES was administered along with the Kaufman Brief Intelligence Test (K-BIT) and the Wechsler Intelligence Scale for Children (WISC-III). The GES was found to correlate significantly with the WISC-III Verbal Scale ($r = .42$), but *negatively* with the Performance Scale ($r = -.37$), and no relationship was found with the overall WISC-III Full Scale IQ or the K-BIT (Levinson, & Folino, 1994). Although the manual reports solid reliability, there is less evidence for substantial validity (Center for Creative Learning, 2002d). Smith (1998), although praising the ease of administration, criticizes the sampling methods. Young (1998) argues that, although the revision is an improvement over the initial version, it still cannot be recommended. The Meeker Creativity Rating Scale (Meeker, 1987) is based on Guilford's Structure of the Intellect model; there is insufficient information on validity and reliability (Center for Creative Learning, 2002c). Another popular scale is the Preschool and Kindergarten Interest Descriptor (Rimm, 1983). Other such scales are discussed on the Center for Creative Learning's website: http://www.creativelearning.com/AssessingCreativity.htm.

GUIDELINES FOR USING CREATIVITY CHECKLISTS

It is of course crucial that the assessors be familiar with the students whose creativity is being rated. They should have had an opportunity to observe the work of the students being assessed in different contexts and working in different domains. The validity of these kinds of assessments depends on many things:

- how well the assessors know the students being assessed
- how well the assessors understand the questions asked and the theory of creativity that underlies them
- the objectivity of the assessors
- the appropriateness of the questions asked and the theory of creativity that underlies them.

With so many variables influencing validity, most of which are beyond the control of those who have developed the checklists, it is understandably difficult to demonstrate validity across wide and diverse samples. No creativity checklist has been able to conduct the kinds of criterion-related concurrent and predictive validity tests one would like to have before using the tests for decision-making purposes.

It is generally helpful if several knowledgeable people can independently rate students, although this is often difficult because of the need for great familiarity with all of the students. If different raters are rating different students' creativity (e.g., if each classroom teacher is rating the creativity of his or her students) and these ratings will then be pooled, one must be aware of possible response set biases in which different raters might consistently rate students higher or lower than others. There is no simple way to control this. One could equalize scores in some way (such as finding the mean for each rater and using transformed scores based on points above or below that mean), but this assumes that the groups of students rated by each rater are equal in overall creativity, which may be a false assumption, especially with small groups.

Creativity checklists generally ask about characteristics, traits, or abilities believed by the checklist creator to be related to creativity in general, not to creativity in specific domains. If one is interested in more domain-specific creativity (e.g., for admission to a program in creative writing), one would probably learn less from a creativity checklist than from something more targeted, such as (in the case of a creative writing program) ratings of the creativity of samples of applicants' writing.

DON'T FORGET

Creativity checklists generally lack sufficient validity to be used alone as measures of creativity, but they can contribute to an overall assessment that uses many other sources of information.

Creativity checklists completed by others, whether they be teachers, parents, or peers, should rarely be used alone as a measure of creativity because they generally lack sufficient validity to allow high-stakes decisions of any kind. As Torrance (2000) advised, in discussing checklists and rating scales as instruments for assessing the creativity of young children:

> These instruments often have strong intuitive appeal but frequently lack the appropriate psychometric properties of validity and reliability. . . . [T]hey cannot be used as exclusive means of identification.

> They can, however, serve as one small piece of an assessment program that when combined with other measures like divergent thinking tests, self-assessment checklists, and ratings of the creativity of artifacts (judged using the Consensual Assessment Technique) can help paint a richer picture of a student's creative abilities.

🖋 TEST YOURSELF 🖋

1. **Assessments of creativity by others generally focus on which of the following?**

   (a) Global assessments of creativity

   (b) Domain-specific creativity

   (c) Creativity of artifacts created for the assessment

2. **Creativity checklists should be made by which of the following?**

   (a) People who do not know the people being assessed and have never observed them

   (b) People who do not know the people being assessed but have observed them

   (c) People who know the people being assessed very well

3. **Assessments of creativity by others are often biased by which of the following?**

   (a) How well the raters like the people being assessed

   (b) Varying concepts of creativity among raters

   (c) The appropriateness of the questions included in the checklist

   (d) All of the above

4. **Assessment by others is superficially similar to the Consensual Assessment Technique (CAT) because:**

   (a) both focus on specific products which judges are asked to evaluate

   (b) both involve creativity ratings by other people

   (c) both focus on global assessments of creativity

5. **Which of the following is NOT a creativity checklist item that is generally highly associated with creativity?**

   (a) Risk-taking behavior

   (b) Independent thinking

   (c) Dependability

   (d) Impulsivity

Answers: 1. a; 2. c; 3. d; 4. b; 5. c

Five

SELF ASSESSMENT

In Chapter Four, we discussed how creativity can be measured by having someone rated—by the creative individual's parents, by her teachers, or by her peers. On the surface, such measurement appears fairly straightforward. Yet out of all of the ways one can measure creativity, perhaps the simplest way is to just ask people how creative they are. It sounds easy and maybe a little too good to be true, and to a certain extent it is. A lot depends on your reasons for wanting to test someone's creativity.

Self-assessment or self-report measures can range from a single question to a handful of questions that can be quickly answered to a full battery of questions that tap into different aspects of creativity.

CREATIVE PERSONALITY ASSESSMENT

Perhaps the most prevalent forms of self-assessment are found in personality inventories. One of the leading theories of personality is the five-factor theory and its variants (Goldberg, 1992; Hofstee, de Raad, & Goldberg, 1992; McCrae & Costa, 1997). These five fac-

DON'T FORGET

The Five-Factor theory of personality includes neuroticism, extraversion, conscientiousness, agreeableness, and openness to experience. Creativity is most associated with openness to experience.

tors are neuroticism (or emotional stability), extraversion, openness to experience (sometimes just called openness), conscientiousness, and agreeableness. The factors are explained in Table 5.1.

The personality factor most associated with creativity is openness to experience. The factor is split into several underlying facets: openness to fantasy (having a good imagination), aesthetics (being artistic), feelings (being emotional and excitable), actions (trying new things and having many interests), ideas (being curious, smart, and liking challenges), and values (being unconventional and liberal). Some of these subcomponents seem less obviously related to creativity. For example, some people who are high on openness to experience in the actions category will like eating new foods or learning a new language. It makes sense that a person like this will be creative, but the connection is less direct because the actions subcomponent seems more related to sensation seeking and risk taking than creativity. Values and feelings are intuitively related to creativity but the connection is again less obvious (there are many creative people who are straitlaced, calm, and conservative). The connection between creativity and openness to fantasy and

Table 5.1

Factor Name	Description
Extraversion	Being outgoing and sociable
Openness/Openness to Experience	Having intellectual and experiential curiosity
Conscientiousness	Being disciplined and rule-oriented and having integrity
Agreeableness	Being friendly and good-natured
Neuroticism/Emotional Stability	Having emotional stability (or lack thereof)

aesthetics is relatively direct, as people most often think of the fantastic and the artistic as creative endeavors.

EVIDENCE FOR VALIDITY

Given the number of subscales related to creative ability, it is therefore unsurprising that there is a near-universal finding that openness to experience is related to a wide variety of creativity measures, such as self-reports of creative acts (Griffin & McDermott, 1998), verbal creativity (King, McKee-Walker, & Broyles, 1996), being in a creative profession (Domino, 1974), analysis of participants' daydreams (Zhiyan & Singer, 1996), creativity ratings on stories (Wolfradt & Pretz, 2001), creative activities and behaviors throughout life (Soldz & Vaillant, 1999), self-estimates of creativity (Furnham, 1999), and psychometric tests (Mc-Crae, 1987). This relationship has been found in an extensive longitudinal study as well. Being a tolerant person, which would seem to be intuitively consistent with being open to new experience, was assessed in individuals at age 27 and then found to be predictive of creative accomplishments at the age of 72 (Feist & Barron, 2003).

Scoring high on open to experience may also be related to high productivity in creative people. King et al. (1996) found that people who were creative and high on the open to experience factor were more likely to report creative accomplishments whereas those who were creative and low on the open to experience factor showed comparatively few creative accomplishments.

This general finding of the power of openness to experience seems to extend across domains. Feist's (1998) extensive meta-analysis of personality and creativity showed that creative scientists were more open to experience than less-creative scientists, and that artists were more open to experience than non-artists.

McCrae (1987) looked at the subcomponents and their relationship to several different divergent thinking measures (mostly looking at some aspect of fluency). All subcomponents were significantly correlated to these measures, and the smallest correlation was found for actions. These relationships, although weakened, stayed significant even when McCrae controlled for vocabulary scores and years of education.

Perrine and Brodersen (2005) examined openness to experience, interests, and artistic versus scientific creativity through a battery of survey measures. Five of the six subcomponents were related to artistic creativity—all but values—with the strongest relationship found in aesthetics. Ideas and values were the only subcomponents related to scientific creativity.

Other factors are related to creativity, if less directly. The research on conscientiousness and creativity, for example, shows a strong domain effect: Creativity in the arts is negatively related to conscientiousness (i.e., creative artists tend to not be conscientious). This finding has been consistent across creativity ratings on stories (Wolfradt & Pretz, 2001) and in biographical data (Walker, Koestner, & Hum, 1995). Students who scored higher on an arts-based creativity measure were also less conscientious (Furnham, Zhang, & Chamorro-Premuzic, 2005). Additionally, Kaufman (2002) found that creative writers were less conscientious than journalists, and Feist's (1998) meta-analysis found that artists were less conscientious than non-artists. There may be a possible interaction between openness to experience and conscientiousness; among people who are high in openness to experience, conscientiousness may reduce creativity as scored in a test of fluency (Ross, 1999).

Feist (1998) also found that although scientists were much more conscientious than non-scientists, creative scientists were not necessarily more conscientious than less-creative scientists. He found few studies suggesting a link between low conscientiousness and high creativity in scientists; the effect in those studies, however, was notably strong. George and Zhou (2001) found that both conscientiousness and openness to experience varied in their relationship to creativity in organizations depending on such factors as a supervisor's feedback and how open-ended a task was.

The NEO Personality Inventory and the briefer NEO Five-Factor Inventory (Costa & McCrae, 1992) are the most popular measures of the five-factor personality theory. Recently, however, Goldberg and colleagues (Goldberg, 1999; Goldberg et al., 2006) have provided free, publicly accessible personality tests that correlate strongly to existing commercial tests. These tests comprise the International Personality Item Pool and are available at http://ipip.ori.org/. As an example, here are five positively keyed items and five negatively keyed items for "imagination":

Positively Keyed
- Have a vivid imagination.
- Prefer variety to routine.
- Believe in the importance of art.
- Enjoy wild flights of fantasy.
- Need a creative outlet.

Negatively Keyed
- Do not like art.
- Do not enjoy going to art museums.
- Do not like poetry.
- Seldom get lost in thought.
- Seldom daydream.

These types of items have been used in many studies (in part due to the site being both user-friendly and free); these personality-based measures of creativity have been used to study such diverse topics as time pressure (Baer & Oldham, 2006), the GREs (Powers & Kaufman, 2004), actors (Nettle, 2006), and differences across domains (Kaufman & Baer, 2004).

There tend to be no differences on any personality factors across cultures (e.g., Goldberg, Sweeney, Merenda, & Hughes, 1998; Kyllonen, Walters, & Kaufman, 2005; McCrae & Costa, 1997). However, Heuchert, Parker, Stumpf, and Myburgh (2000) found that White South Africans scored higher on openness to experience than Black South Africans (although it is important to note much of this difference was in the openness to feelings subcomponent, as opposed to the more creativity-related openness to fantasy and aesthetics subcomponents). Allik and McCrae (2004) found that people from European and European-American cultures tended to be more open to experience than people from Asian and African cultures. Schmitt, Allik, McCrae, and Benet-Martínez (in press), in a massive study of 17,837 people from 56 nations, found that people from South American and European countries were significantly the most open to experience, with people from South Asian countries generally being less open to experience. African countries were in the middle. It is worth pointing out, in addition, that Saucier and Goldberg (2001) studied personality labels in 13 languages (including English) and found that openness to experience was the only one of the Big Five (in addition to emotional stability, extraversion, conscientiousness, and agreeableness) to *not* be found in all languages. Openness to experience, therefore, can be considered specific to Anglo cultures (Benet-Martinez & Oishi, in press).

CREATIVITY STYLES

Creativity styles are similar to personality; they refer to the ways in which people choose to use their creativity (Houtz et al., 2003; Isaksen & Dorval, 1993; Selby, Treffinger, Isaksen, & Powers, 1993). The Creativity Styles Questionnaire-Revised (Kumar, Kemmler, & Holman, 1997; see also Kumar & Holman, 1989) is a 76-item self-assessed questionnaire with seven subscales (see Table 5.2).

Table 5.2 Examples of Items from the Creativity Styles Questionnaire-Revised

Subscale	Sample Item
Belief in the Unconscious Process	I have had insights, the sources of which I am unable to explain or understand.
Use of Techniques	I typically create new ideas by combining existing ideas.
Use of Other People	When I get stuck, I consult or talk with people about how to proceed.
Final Product Orientation	I enjoy the process of creating new ideas when they lead to a final product or not.
Superstition	I have a favorite amulet or clothing that I wear when I am engaged in creative work.
Environmental Control	I have set aside a particular place (or places) for creative work.
Uses of the Senses	I tend to use all of my visual sense a lot in my work.

Source: Adapted from Kumar, Kemmler, & Holman, 1997.

Kumar, Holman, and Rudegeair (1991) looked at the original Creative Styles Questionnaire and found that more creative students used more techniques and were less guided by the goal of a final product (this finding is consistent with a large section of motivation literature; see Agars, Kaufman, & Locke, in press; Amabile, 1996; Ruscio, Whitney, & Amabile, 1998). Kumar et al. (1997) found similar results with the Creative Styles Questionnaire-Revised, with the added finding that students who were more creative were likely to believe in unconscious processes.

Another measure of creativity styles is the Kirton Adaption-Innovation Inventory (KAI; Kirton, 1999), which is primarily intended for use by organizations. The KAI is based on Kirton's (1994b) Adaption-Innovation Theory of cognitive styles, which deals primarily with styles as they apply to cognitive activities involving creativity and problem solving. Stated briefly, Adaption-Innovation Theory proposes that,

> [A] critical characteristic of the habitual *adaptor* when confronting a problem is to accept the generally recognized theories, policies, customary viewpoints or . . . paradigms in which it appears to be embedded. By contrast, the characteristic style of the habitual *innovator* is eventually to detach the problem from its cocoon of accepted thought, to reconstruct the problem and its attendant paradigm whilst in the pursuit of a solution. (Kirton, 1994b, p. 8, emphasis added)

Although Kirton notes that "the innovative approach is obviously needed in any organization that is to survive" (p. 9), he also acknowledges that the adaptive approach is necessary for long-term success (especially for large organizations) in order to mediate risk. The purpose of the KAI is to provide "a score that distinguishes operationally adaptors and innovators on a continuum".

As reported in Kirton (1994a), the KAI is a 32-item assessment that produces a score that can range from 32 to 160 (although the observed range has been reported as 45 to 146) with an average of 96 and a distribution approaching normality. Differences among samples from six industrialized countries are minute, and stability and internal consistency estimates are generally above .80. Evidence of construct validity is also generally positive. The KAI items measuring originality have been found to correlate significantly with measures of self-esteem (Goldsmith, 1985; Goldsmith & Matherly, 1988) and creative self-perception (Houtz et al., 2003).

CREATIVITY AND INTERESTS

Research on interests is closely related to the work done in personality. Holland's (1997) model of vocational interests includes six categories: realistic, investigative, artistic, social, enterprising, and conventional. Holland's extensive self-report data suggested that artistic interests were most related to creativity (again, an intuitive connection), followed by investigative, social, and enterprising interests in that order (realistic and conventional interests are not particularly associated with creativity). Helson

Rapid Reference 5.1

Overview of the Relationship between Personality Assessments and Creativity

- Most common personality theory has five factors: neuroticism (emotional stability), extraversion, openness to experience, conscientiousness, and agreeableness.

- Openness to experience is the most related to creativity.

- Subcomponents of openness to experience are openness to fantasy, aesthetics, feelings, actions, ideas, and values.

and colleagues (1996; Helson, Roberts, & Agronick, 1995) developed an Occupational Creativity Scale based on Holland's work. They found that a variety of creativity measures given to women at age 21 (including self-reports of imaginative and artistic interests in childhood) were correlated to occupational creativity at age 52. Perrine and Brodersen (2005) found that artistic interests predict artistic creativity and investigative interests predict scientific creativity. (See Rapid Reference 5.1.)

SELF-ESTIMATED CREATIVITY

Even more direct than asking people to self-assess their personality, interests, or styles is to simply ask them outright to rate their own creativity. A typical question might ask, "Rate your creativity on a scale from

1 to 10." Another format is to show a picture of a typical IQ bell curve and ask, "Using a scale with 100 being average, rate your own creativity." Although these types of questions are often incorporated into larger questionnaires, surprisingly few studies have specifically examined self-estimated creativity. Furnham and his colleagues (Furnham, 1999; Furnham, Zhang, & Chamorro-Premuzic, 2006) asked students to assess their own creativity and administered the Barron Welsh Art Scale and a Five Factor personality test. They found that self-assessed creativity was significantly related to creativity as measured by the Barron Welsh Art Scale. They also found that self-assessed creativity was correlated with conscientiousness (although the correlation with openness to experience missed significance).

Kaufman and Baer (2004) asked 241 college students to rate their creativity in nine areas—science, interpersonal relationships, writing, art, interpersonal communication, solving personal problems, mathematics, crafts, and bodily/physical movement. A three-factor solution emerged, with creativity in empathy/communication (creativity in the areas of interpersonal relationships, communication, solving personal problems, and writing); "Hands On" creativity (art, crafts, and bodily/kinesthetic creativity); and math/science creativity (creativity in math or science). Interestingly, these are similar to three factors found in the area of student motivation—writing, art, and problem solving (Ruscio, Whitney, & Amabile, 1998). A study of Turkish undergraduates found a slightly different factor structure, with an arts factor (art, writing, crafts), an empathy/communication factor (interpersonal relationships, communication, solving personal problems), and a math/science factor (math, science). Bodily/kinesthetic creativity was not associated with any of the three factors (Oral, Kaufman, & Agars, 2007).

Kaufman, Cole, and Baer

CAUTION

Differences across domains should be taken into account. People may evaluate themselves in different ways depending on the domain.

(in press) expanded the investigation into self-reported creativity across domains by asking participants to rate their own creativity on 56 domains in the Creativity Domain Questionnaire. With data on more than 3,500 participants, seven factors emerged: artistic-verbal, artistic-visual, entrepreneur, interpersonal, math/science, performance, and problem solving. These seven factors were found as hierarchical second-order factors. In other words, just as some theorists argue for a single construct of intelligence ("g"), there is some evidence for an analogous single construct of creativity ("c"). However, such a single construct is only part of the broader picture. It is interesting to note that some general thematic areas were strongly related to the "c" factor (i.e., overall creativity). Performance and artistic/visual were strongly related, whereas math/science was the least related to self-perceived overall creativity.

One hypothesis states that mathematics and science may not fall into people's conceptions of creativity (Kaufman & Baer, 2004; Kaufman, et al., in press); that is, the average person may not consider areas such as math or science when defining what it means to be creative. This idea is consistent with Paulos's (1988) idea of innumeracy, the inability to accurately use numbers and chance. "Romantic misconceptions about the nature of mathematics," Paulos wrote, "lead to an intellectual environment hospitable to and even encouraging of poor mathematical education and psychological distaste for the subject and lie at the base of much innumeracy" (1988, p. 120). The implication here is that people may be mathematically averse and prone to misconceiving mathematics as a cold, mechanical domain in which creativity is neither needed nor welcome nor useful. Nothing could be further from the truth, of course, but this logic—or lack thereof—may explain some of the results on the CDQ and related measures.

Figure 5.1 shows the Creative Domains Questionnaire. After each item we include how the item is coded in parenthesis, with the coding being as follows: VER = artistic-verbal; VIS = artistic-visual; ENT = entrepreneur; IP = interpersonal; MS = math/science; PER = performance; and PS = problem solving (PS).

*Please rate your **creativity** in the following domains. Some of these domains may seem to overlap. Do not worry about this; rather, try to think about your creativity in each specific domain as you understand it, without worrying about how it may overlap with other domains listed. For domains that you are not personally familiar with, feel free to check "Not Applicable." Thank you!*

How creative are you in:

	Not Applicable	Not at all creative	Not very creative	A little creative	Somewhat creative	Very creative	Extremely creative
Accounting/Money Management (ENT)	O	O	O	O	O	O	O
Acting/Performance (PER)	O	O	O	O	O	O	O
Advertising/Sales (ENT)	O	O	O	O	O	O	O
Algebra/Trigonometry (MS)	O	O	O	O	O	O	O
Architecture/Design (VIS)	O	O	O	O	O	O	O
Ballet/Dance/Gymnastics/Creative Movement (PER)	O	O	O	O	O	O	O
Business/Entrepreneurial Abilities (ENT)	O	O	O	O	O	O	O
Chemistry (MS)	O	O	O	O	O	O	O
Computers/Computer Science (MS)	O	O	O	O	O	O	O
Cooking (IP)	O	O	O	O	O	O	O
Crafts/Sculpture/"Folk" Art (VIS)	O	O	O	O	O	O	O
Earth Sciences (MS)	O	O	O	O	O	O	O

Figure 5.1. Creative Domains Questionnaire

Source: Adapted from Kaufman, 2006; Kaufman, Cole, & Baer, 2008.

	Not Applicable	Not at all creative	Not very creative	A little creative	Somewhat creative	Very creative	Extremely creative
Emotions (IP)	O	O	O	O	O	O	O
English Literature/Criticism (VER)	O	O	O	O	O	O	O
Fashion/Working with Clothing (PER)	O	O	O	O	O	O	O
Film and/or Theatrical Writing/Direction (PER)	O	O	O	O	O	O	O
Geometry (MS)	O	O	O	O	O	O	O
Graphic Design/Multimedia (VIS)	O	O	O	O	O	O	O
History/Historical Analysis (MS)	O	O	O	O	O	O	O
Horticulture/Gardening (VIS)	O	O	O	O	O	O	O
Humor/Comedy (IP)	O	O	O	O	O	O	O
Interacting/Communicating with Children (IP)	O	O	O	O	O	O	O
Interacting/Communicating with Friends and Family (IP)	O	O	O	O	O	O	O
Interacting/Communicating with Strangers (IP)	O	O	O	O	O	O	O
Interior Design/Decorating (VIS)	O	O	O	O	O	O	O
Law/Legal Skills (PS)	O	O	O	O	O	O	O
Life Sciences/Biology (MS)	O	O	O	O	O	O	O
Logic/Puzzles/"Everyday Math" (PS)	O	O	O	O	O	O	O

Figure 5.1. (continued)

	Not Applicable	Not at all creative	Not very creative	A little creative	Somewhat creative	Very creative	Extremely creative
Mechanical Abilities (PS)	O	O	O	O	O	O	O
Medicine (MS)	O	O	O	O	O	O	O
Music Composition (PER)	O	O	O	O	O	O	O
Naturalistic Science/Resource Management (MS)	O	O	O	O	O	O	O
Painting/Drawing (VIS)	O	O	O	O	O	O	O
Personnel Management/Leadership (ENT)	O	O	O	O	O	O	O
Photography (VIS)	O	O	O	O	O	O	O
Physics (MS)	O	O	O	O	O	O	O
Playing a Musical Instrument (PER)	O	O	O	O	O	O	O
Political Sciences (inc. Economics) (MS)	O	O	O	O	O	O	O
Problem Solving (PS)	O	O	O	O	O	O	O
Psychotherapy/Psychiatry (IP)	O	O	O	O	O	O	O
Social Sciences (inc. Psychology, Anthropology, Sociology) (IP)	O	O	O	O	O	O	O
Solving Personal Problems (IP)	O	O	O	O	O	O	O

Figure 5.1. (continued)

	Not Applicable	Not at all creative	Not very creative	A little creative	Somewhat creative	Very creative	Extremely creative
Spatial-Visual Abilities (VIS)	O	O	O	O	O	O	O
Speech/Debate/Verbal Abilities (VER)	O	O	O	O	O	O	O
Spirituality/Religious Thought (IP)	O	O	O	O	O	O	O
Sports Performance (PER)	O	O	O	O	O	O	O
Sports Strategy (PS)	O	O	O	O	O	O	O
Teaching/Education (IP)	O	O	O	O	O	O	O
Textiles/Fabrics (VIS)	O	O	O	O	O	O	O
Travel/Interacting with Different Cultures (IP)	O	O	O	O	O	O	O
Vocal Performance/Singing (PER)	O	O	O	O	O	O	O
Wood/Metal Working (VIS)	O	O	O	O	O	O	O
Working with Animals/Animal Training and Management (IP)	O	O	O	O	O	O	O
Writing Fiction/Prose (VER)	O	O	O	O	O	O	O
Writing Non-Fiction/Journalism (VER)	O	O	O	O	O	O	O
Writing Poetry (VER)	O	O	O	O	O	O	O

Figure 5.1. (continued)

Traditionally, males rate themselves as more creative than females (Furnham, 1999; Furnham et al., 2006; Kaufman, 2006), although some studies have found no differences (Chan, 2005; Goldsmith & Matherly, 1988). Kaufman's (2006) analysis of ethnic differences across the 56 domains revealed that African Americans rated themselves as significantly higher than at least one other ethnicity on all factors. All ethnicities except for Asian Americans rated themselves higher than another ethnicity on at least one factor. Plucker, Runco, and Lim (2006) found no difference in creative potential between Korean students and American students; similarly, Lim and Plucker (2001) found that Koreans and Americans hold very similar concepts about the nature of creativity. Malaysian students scored higher than American, Indian, and Hungarian students on one self-report measure of creativity, but American students scored higher than Malaysian students on a different self-report measure (Palaniappan, 1996).

EVIDENCE FOR VALIDITY

Self-report measures tend to correlate highly with each other (e.g., Fleenor & Taylor, 1994; Goldsmith & Matherly; Kaufman & Baer, 2004), although self-report measures do not appear to correlate highly with self-reported creative activities (Eisenman & Grove, 1972). Studies that examine self-report measures of creativity with performance or psychometric measures of creativity have been inconsistent. Furnham's studies, as discussed earlier, lend support for a connection between self-assessed and psychometric creativity (1999; Furnam, Zhang, & Chamorro-Premuzic, 2006). Yet Lee, Day, Meara, and Maxwell (2002) used three measures of creativity (verbal, pictorial, and self-report) and found little relationship among the three measures. Priest (2006) found that students' self-assessment of the creativity of their musical compositions was not predictive of expert ratings of these same compositions. Park, Lee, and Hahn (2002), however, found self-reported creativity to significantly correlate with all scores on the Torrance Tests of Creative Thinking except for fluency, and Phillips (1972) found that self-assessments did differ between high-scorers on the TTCT and low-scorers.

It is interesting to note that self-assessments are more on-target when people rate their intelligence. The correlations between perceived and actual intelligence typically range from .30 to .50 (e.g., Chamorro-Premuzic, Furnham, & Moutafi, 2004; Furnham & Chamorro-Premuzic, 2004; Paulhus, Lysy, & Yik, 1998).

The evidence of validity for self-reports of creativity should be considered in light of the growing research on people's apparently limited ability to judge their abilities and performance accurately (Dunning, 2005; Dunning, Johnson, Ehrlinger, & Kruger, 2003; Kruger, 1999). This limitation appears to be especially profound when assessing areas in which one has low levels of skill or capability (Kruger & Dunning, 1999). Taken collectively, the general research on competence, the validity evidence on self-reports, and recent studies on self-evaluation of creativity suggest that people are not accurate judges of highly creative ideas (evaluating them to be more common than they actually are) and less creative ideas (judging them to be more original than they actually are). However, more research is clearly needed on this topic.

CREATIVE BEHAVIOR CHECKLISTS

A creative behavior checklist asks people to rate past creative accomplishments, rather than asking questions related to personality. These checklists typically ask participants to report past accomplishments (e.g., King, McKee, & Broyles, 1996), although some also ask about current or past activities.

Hocevar, author of the Creative Behavior Inventory (1979), has ar-

DON'T FORGET
....
Creative behavior checklists usually ask about someone's past accomplishments and activities.

gued that self-reports of activities and attainments are among the best techniques for measuring creativity (1981; Hocevar & Bachelor, 1989). His inventory has 90 items and assesses creative behavior in literature, music, crafts, art, performing arts, and math/science. Plucker (1999b) found evidence that the subscale scores were reliable but tended to collapse onto one strong factor, calling into question their use as separate scores. Dollinger, Burke, and Gump (2007) found that although the Creative Behavior Inventory showed strong reliability, it correlated only .06 (non-significant) with three rated creative products (a drawing, story, and photo essay).

One of the earlier behavioral checklists was the Alpha Biological Inventory (Taylor & Ellison, 1966, 1967). More recent ones include the Creativity Achievement Questionnaire (CAQ; Carson, Peterson, & Higgins, 2005) and the Runco Ideational Behavior Scale (RIBS; Runco, in press).

Ivcevic and Mayer (2007) used a creative activities checklist in combination with a personality inventory to derive five "types": conventional, everyday creative individuals, artists, scholars, and renaissance individuals.

The CAQ (Carson et al., 2005) assesses creativity with 96 items across 10 domains that load on two factors: the arts (drama, writing, humor, music, visual arts, and dance) and science (invention, science, and culinary). The tenth domain, architecture, did not load on a factor. The CAQ was shown to have test-retest reliability (.81) and internal consistency reliability (.96) in 117 students. Carson et al. (2005) demonstrated validity in smaller samples, with significant correlations between CAQ scores and rated artwork, divergent thinking tasks, and openness to experience scores. A typical set of items on the CAQ is:

Humor

0. I do not have recognized talent in this area (Skip to next question).
1. People have often commented on my original sense of humor.
2. I have created jokes that are now repeated by others.
3. I have written jokes for other people.
4. I have written a joke or cartoon that has been published.
5. I have worked as a professional comedian.
6. I have worked as a professional comedy writer.
7. My humor has been recognized in a national publication.

The item would be scored by assigning the number of points next to the question (0–7) to a person to indicate creativity in that area (taken from Carson et al., 2005).

We will discuss the RIBS as an example of a typical behavior checklist. The RIBS was developed in response to Runco's (in press) perceived need for a more appropriate criterion in studies of predictive validity for divergent thinking tests. As noted earlier (see Chapter Two), research on the predictive validity of divergent thinking tests is mixed. Runco posited that one explanation for these unconvincing results is that researchers were using divergent thinking tests to predict inappropriate criteria, such as those traditionally used in studies of the predictive validity of intelligence or achievement tests. Runco reasoned that a more appropriate criterion would be one that emphasizes ideation: the use of, appreciation of, and skill of generating ideas.

In earlier work on creative behavioral checklists, Runco (1986b) asked 150 elementary school children to rate their creativity on 65 questions across seven domains (writing, music, crafts, art, science, performing arts, and public presentation). He found solid reliability scores for both quantity and quality of contributions. Runco, Plucker, and Lim (2001) created a pool of 100 items that, after initial pilot testing, was reduced to 23 items. All of the items describe actual overt behavior related to ideation. Items include:

1. I have many wild ideas.
2. I think about ideas more often than most people.
3. I often get excited by my own new ideas.
4. I come up with a lot of ideas or solutions to problems.
5. I come up with an idea or solution other people have never thought of.
6. I like to play around with ideas for the fun of it.
7. It is important to be able to think of bizarre and wild possibilities.
8. I would rate myself highly in being able to come up with ideas.
9. I have always been an active thinker; I have lots of ideas.
10. I enjoy having leeway in the things I do and room to make up my own mind.
11. My ideas are often considered impractical or even wild.
12. I would take a college course based on original ideas.
13. I am able to think about things intensely for many hours.
14. Sometimes I get so interested in a new idea that I forget about other things that I should be doing.
15. I often have trouble sleeping at night, because so many ideas keep popping into my head.
16. When writing papers or talking to people, I often have trouble staying with one topic because I think of so many things to write or say.
17. I often find that one of my ideas has led me to other ideas which have led me to other ideas, and I end up with an idea and do not know where it came from.

18. Some people might think me scatter brained or absent minded because I think about a variety of things at once.
19. I try to exercise my mind by thinking things through.
20. I am able to think up answers to problems that haven't already been figured out.
21. I am good at combining ideas in ways that others have not tried.
22. Friends ask me to help them think of ideas and solutions.
23. I have ideas about new inventions or about how to improve things.

Runco, Plucker, and Lim (2000, 2001), using a sample of 321 college students from three universities (97 in the first sample and 224 in a comparison sample), investigated the RIBS' psychometric integrity. The internal consistency estimates were satisfactory for both samples ($\alpha_1 = .92$, $\alpha_2 = .91$). To gather evidence of construct validity, Runco and his colleagues applied factor analysis to the data using principal axis factoring. They determined that a one-factor model fit the data effectively; this was consistent with the unitary theoretical construct on which the instrument was based. Runco et al. used confirmatory factor analysis with bootstrapping to gather evidence related to the generalizability of the factor structures obtained for the first sample's data. Results suggested that a one-factor model with correlated uniquenesses and a two correlated factors model with correlated uniquenesses had the best degree of fit to the data. However, the difference in fit between the two models was small. Runco et al. concluded that the RIBS was a sufficiently reliable instrument for use with groups and individuals, but that the construct validity evidence was somewhat ambiguous. Given the lack of a theoretical justification for the presence of two factors and the high correlation between factors in the two-factor solutions, Runco et al. suggested that the one-factor structure should guide interpretation of RIBS results.

CREATIVE SELF-EFFICACY

Creative self-efficacy refers to self-judgments and personal identification with being creative. Much of the research on creative self-efficacy is rooted in the concept of self-efficacy (one's beliefs about one's own abilities; see Bandura, 1997). Tierney and Farmer (2002), building on work by Gist and Mitchell (1992), proposed the concept of creative self-efficacy as representing a person's beliefs about how creative he or she can be. These beliefs are often rooted in a situational or narrow context (e.g., Jaussi, Randel, & Dionne, 2007). A broader view of creative self-efficacy examines creative personal identity, which is also reflective of how much someone values creativity (e.g., Randel & Jaussi, 2003).

Measures of creative self-efficacy are often brief; as an example, Beghetto (2006) used a three-item scale, with a reliability alpha of .86. His scale asked students to rate their agreement with these three statements:

- I am good at coming up with new ideas.
- I have a lot of good ideas.
- I have a good imagination.

Other examples include "I have confidence in my ability to solve problems creatively" from the work of Tierney and Farmer (2002). Jaussi et al. (2007) used the following questions to measure creative personal identity, with a reliability alpha of .89:

- In general, my creativity is an important part of my self-image.
- My creativity is an important part of who I am.
- Overall, my creativity has little to do with who I am. (reverse coded)

- My ability to be creative is an important reflection of who I am.

Creative self-efficacy has been shown to relate to receiving teacher feedback on creativity (Beghetto, 2006), to creative organizational performance (Tierney & Farmer, 2002), and the ability to apply situations to new contexts (Jaussi et al., 2007). There are legitimate questions, however, about the differentiation between measures of creative self-efficacy and instruments such as the RIBS, which have similar items but are intended to measure different—but related—constructs. This is clearly an area in need of additional theoretical and psychometric development.

SUMMING UP

Self-reported creativity, whether via a creative personality test, self-assessment, or related measure, is particularly attractive because it is typically quick, easy to score, and intuitive (who knows your creativity better than you do?). Two cautions are needed, however. The first caution, as discussed in this chapter, is that the validity for these assessments is highly inconsistent. Although self-assessments often correlate to each other, they are spottier about correlating to performance-based assessments. The second caution is that, just as television's Dr. House says, "Everybody lies." Although self-assessments have a function and purpose, they are not useful in any type of high-stakes assessment. If testing is taking place to see if a person will be hired, accepted by a university or college, receive a scholarship, or enjoy some other positive outcome, then he or she may be motivated to give the answers that will be self-beneficial. Thus, although self-assessments have a function and purpose, they are not useful in any type of high-stakes assessment. Most self-reported measures of creativity are easily deciphered by the layman. On one hand, this transparency offers high face validity. On the other hand, they are easy to cheat on. Measures of self-reported creativity are only recommended if the person being tested has no clear ulterior purpose to lie. If you develop a brief measure of self-rated creativity for your own use in assessing people, you should try to include some items that are not entirely obvious, and items that are both indicative and counter-indicative.

🐿 TEST YOURSELF 🐿

1. **The personality factor most associated with creativity is**
   (a) extraversion
   (b) openness to experience
   (c) conscientiousness

2. **When people evaluate their own creativity across domains, which area is least associated with their general concept of their creativity?**
   (a) Poetry
   (b) Interacting with People
   (c) Math

3. **Creative self-efficacy refers to:**
   (a) how creativity your friends think you are
   (b) your personal definition of creativity
   (c) how creativity you think you are

4. **One danger of self-assessment measures is that**
   (a) people may overestimate their own creativity
   (b) such measures lack face validity
   (c) some people may confuse creativity and emotional intelligence

5. **The Kirton Adaption-Innovation Inventory considers creativity to be a**

   (a) Cognitive style

   (b) Motivational Trait

   (c) Biological Factor

6. **Generally, who rates themselves as being more creative, males or females?**

Answers: 1-b, 2-c, 3-c, 4-a, 5-a, 6-males

Six

CREATIVITY, INTELLIGENCE, AND GIFTEDNESS

A s noted earlier, the potential relationship between creativity and many other constructs is of great interest to many people. For example, is a person with high levels of creativity more or less likely to be intelligent or wise? What is the relationship between creativity and social skills, especially the ability to solve problems via social interaction? How does creativity relate to success in school, on the athletic field, or in the boardroom? Because creativity, specifically the ability to solve problems creatively, is so universally useful, its relationship to any construct or aspect of human life is worthy of study.

From an assessment perspective, the relationship of creativity to both intelligence and giftedness is of particular interest. First, the overlap (or lack thereof) between intelligence and creativity is enduringly popular, controversial, and heavily dependent on psychometric issues. Second, creativity plays a major role in several theories of giftedness, and school districts struggle with the development of systems to identify gifted students, especially those with above-average creative abilities. The purpose of this chapter is to review recent research on creativity, intelligence, and giftedness, and we highlight a number of practical issues that emerge from the research and have a specific impact on creativity assessment.

CREATIVITY AND INTELLIGENCE

Creativity and intelligence, like chocolate and peanut butter, certainly *seem* like they should go together. Indeed, Sternberg and O'Hara (1999) have argued that the relationship "is theoretically important, and its answer probably affects the lives of countless children and adults" (p. 269). Their point is well-taken: Psychologists and educators frequently address issues related to either creativity *or* intelligence, but they often ignore the interplay between the two—or worse, they feel intelligence and creativity are inversely related. This may explain why research has consistently shown that teachers prefer intelligent students over creative students, as though students are unlikely to exhibit evidence of high levels of both constructs. In addition, the nature of the relationship could help identify aspects of each construct that are ignored in traditional classroom settings. For example, Wallach and Kogan (1965) suggested that students with high creativity but low intelligence are more disadvantaged in the traditional classroom setting than students with low creativity and low intelligence.

Regardless of the controversy, Plucker and Renzulli (1999) conclude it is now a matter of uncovering not whether but *how* the two are related. Certainly, creativity has been an important part of many major theories of intelligence. For example, divergent thinking was an integral part of Guilford's (1967) Structure of the Intellect model. But, in general, the research on this topic is murky if not seemingly

> **CAUTION**
>
> Although it seems clear that there is some kind of relationship between intelligence and creativity, the nature of that relationship is murky at best. Creativity has been part of some theories of intelligence, suggesting the two are closely related; it has also been suggested that a certain level of intelligence is necessary for creative performance; and yet there is evidence that very high levels of intelligence might actually interfere with creativity.

in outright conflict. For example, the threshold theory suggests intelligence is a necessary but not a sufficient condition of creativity (Barron, 1969; Yamamoto, 1964a, 1964b), certification theory focuses on environmental factors that allow people to display creativity and intelligence (Hayes, 1989), and an interference hypothesis suggests that very high levels of intelligence may interfere with creativity (Simonton, 1994; Sternberg, 1996).

A FRAMEWORK FOR EXPLORING THE RESEARCH

Sternberg (1999c) has provided a framework for examining the research on this topic. We find this framework to be helpful because it emphasizes that one's conclusions about the creativity-intelligence relationship will largely be determined by her or his theoretical conceptualization of each construct. The Sternberg framework includes five possible intelligence-creativity relationships: creativity as a subset of intelligence; intelligence as a subset of creativity; creativity and intelligence as overlapping sets; creativity and intelligence as coincident sets; and creativity and intelligence as disjoint sets. In the following sections, we provide examples of each type of relationship.[1]

Creativity as a Subset of Intelligence

A number of psychometric theories of intelligence include creativity, either explicitly or implicitly, as a subset of intelligence. Guilford's SOI model is probably the most explicit, with divergent thinking specifically identified as one of his five cognitive operations. This model was influential in educational circles (Meeker, 1969), and Renzulli (1973)

---

1. We do not include discussion of the coincident set and disjoint set categories, which in our view are much less common compared to the other categories and do not reflect current, major lines of inquiry within the field.

developed an entire creativity curriculum based on the aspects of the SOI Model involving divergent thinking. From a very different perspective, Gardner (1993) has applied his Theory of Multiple Intelligences as a lens through which to study highly creative people, implicitly including creativity as a subset of MI Theory.

DON'T FORGET

Guilford included divergent production as one of five cognitive operations. Divergent production is often used as a way to measure some aspects of creativity.

Perhaps the theory of intelligence that is most used in IQ tests is the CHC (Cattell-Horn-Carroll) Theory, a combination of the Cattell-Horn theory of fluid and crystallized intelligence (Horn & Cattell, 1966; Horn & Noll, 1997) and Carroll's Three-Stratum Theory (1993). CHC Theory proposes 10 factors of intelligence (Table 6.1). Creativity/originality is considered one of the components of *Glr*, or long-term storage and retrieval of information. Specific components of *Glr* and their relationship to creativity are discussed in more detail in Kaufman and Kaufman (2008).

The CHC theory has been particularly influential in the development of recent IQ tests, most notably the fifth edition of the Stanford-Binet (Roid, 2003), the Kaufman Assessment Battery for Children – Second Edition (KABC-II; Kaufman & Kaufman, 2004), and the Woodcock-Johnson – Third Edition (WJ-III; Woodcock, McGrew, & Mather, 2001). Largely because of the influence of CHC theory, all current IQ tests (including the Wechsler Intelligence Scale for Children – Fourth Edition; WISC-IV, Wechsler, 2003) have shifted the historical focus from a small number of part scores to a contemporary emphasis on anywhere from four to seven cognitive abilities (Sternberg, Kaufman, & Grigorenko, 2008).

An intriguing and fairly recent perspective in this category is Sternberg's (1996, 1997, 1999c, Sternberg et al., 2008) theory of successful

Table 6.1. Components of the Cattell-Horn-Carroll Theory

Component	Symbol	Description	Example
Fluid intelligence	Gf	Use of a variety of mental operations to solve novel problems (not tasks that can be performed automatically)	Using intuitive or deductive reasoning
Quantitative knowledge	Gq	Use of procedural quantitative knowledge	Completing a basic test of mathematics
Crystallized intelligence	Gc	The breadth and depth of a person's accumulated knowledge of a culture and the ability to use that knowledge to solve problems	Knowledge of grammar
Reading and writing	Grw	Use of reading/writing skills and knowledge	Understanding a paragraph
Short-term memory	Gsm	Remember and retain information from very recent events (i.e., a few minutes)	Ability to keep a series of numbers in one's working memory
Visual processing	Gv	The ability to use and manipulate visual images	Keeping an image briefly in memory
Auditory processing	Ga	The ability to use and manipulate auditory information	Ability to identify the pitch of a tone

Long-term storage and retrieval	Glr	Remember and retain information from long-term memory (i.e., hours, weeks, or more)	Being able to name many different words that fit a category (such as vegetables starting with the letter T)
Processing speed	Gs	Perform automatic tasks rapidly	Reading a specific passage quickly
Decision speed/reaction time	Gt	Ability to react and make decisions in a short space of time	Quickly finding the difference between two different objects
General (domain-specific) knowledge	Gkn	The aspect of acquired knowledge that lies in areas beyond normal cultural knowledge	Knowledge of sign language
Psychomotor speed	Gps	Ability to immediately move one's body	Copying words or making sounds as quickly as possible
Psychomotor abilities	Gp	Abilities to move one's body with strength or grace	Possessing manual dexterity

Source: Adapted from McGrew, 2005. McGrew includes a few other abilities (such as olfactory abilities) that are less commonly studied and are omitted for the sake of space.

intelligence, which includes creative abilities as one of three essential components, along with analytical and practical abilities. Although not currently adapted into a major commercial test, this theory has served as the basis for interesting work in college admissions. The first burst of research was on the Sternberg Triarchic Abilities Test (Level H of the STAT; Sternberg, 1993; see Sternberg & Clinkenbeard, 1995; Sternberg, Grigorenko, Ferrari, & Clinkenbeard, 1999; Sternberg, Ferrari, Clinkenbeard, & Grigorenko, 1996; Sternberg, Torff, & Grigorenko, 1998a, 1998b). Initially, three multiple-choice subtests and three open-ended subtests were included that measured creativity, as are described in Table 6.2.

The open-ended measures were evaluated using a similar methodology as the CAT. Performance was then rated by trained judges for cleverness, humor, originality, and task appropriateness (for the cartoons), and originality, complexity, emotional evocativeness, and descriptiveness for both written and oral stories (Sternberg & Lubart, 1995, 1996). This work has continued being studied and expanded into a large-scale development and testing initiative called the Rainbow Project (see Sternberg & the Rainbow Project Collaborators, 2006). It is important to note that the multiple-choice items are not used anymore; however, the open-ended items are still used in both research and applied settings.

Indeed, Sternberg and his colleagues at Tufts University have added an explicit assessment of creativity (based on his work with the open-ended creativity measures) as a non-required component for college admission. His measures (not only of creativity, but for all components of successful intelligence) predict college success more accurately than standard admissions tests; in addition,

> **DON'T FORGET**
>
> Sternberg's theory of successful intelligence includes creativity as one of three key components (the others being practical and analytical intelligence).

Table 6.2

Test type	Brief description	Example
Creative-Verbal (Multiple Choice)	Solve verbal analogies with false premises, proceeding as if these premises were true.	The ability to use premises such as "money falls off trees."
Creative-Quantitative (Multiple Choice)	Solve novel number operations	Using such techniques as "flix," which entails manipulating numbers that are different based on if the first number is greater than, equal to, or less than the second number.
Creative-Figural (Multiple Choice)	Detect and apply transformations in a series of images	Images that are different in a specific, sequential way are presented to a test-taker, who is then asked to continue these patterns of transformations on a new figure.
Cartoons (Open-Ended)	Write captions to a cartoon	Titles include "The Octopus's Sneakers" and "2983"
Written Stories (Open-Ended)	Write short stories based on unusual titles	Cartoons taken from the New Yorker archive but presented without the captions
Oral Stories (Open-Ended)	Tell a story based on a selection of images	Each set of images revolve around a common theme, such as "keys" or "animals playing music"

Source: Adapted from Sternberg, Grigorenko, Ferrari, and Clinkenbeard, 1999 and Sternberg and the Rainbow Project Collaborators, 2006.

ethnic differences are significantly reduced (Stemler, Grigorenko, Jarvin, & Sternberg, 2006; Sternberg, 2006; Sternberg & the Rainbow Project Collaborators, 2006).

Intelligence as a Subset of Creativity

A less common perspective is that intelligence is a subset of creativity. Perhaps the best recent example of this approach is Sternberg and Lubart's (1995) Investment Theory of Creativity or Amabile's (1996) Componential Theory of Creativity, both of which include intellect (in the Investment Theory, represented by intelligence and knowledge; in the Componential Theory, represented by domain-specific and creativity-general intellectual abilities).

Overlapping Sets

The third category includes conceptualizations where the constructs of intelligence and creativity overlap but remain distinct, with one not subsuming the other. For example, Renzulli's (1978) three-ring conception of giftedness theorizes that giftedness—implicitly cast as high-level creative production—is caused by the overlap of high intellectual ability, creativity, and task commitment. From this perspective, creativity and intelligence are distinct constructs but overlap considerably under the right conditions.

The PASS (Planning, Attention, Simultaneous, and Successive) theory is a cognitive processing theory based on the works of Luria (see Das, Naglieri, & Kirby, 1994, for an overview). Luria's (1966, 1970, 1973) original neuropsychological model featured three Blocks or functional units. According to this model, the first functional unit is responsible for focused attention. The second functional unit receives and stores information with both simultaneous and successive (or sequential) processing. Simultaneous processing is integrating information together;

Table 6.3 Components of the PASS Model

Functional Unit	Description	Example
Planning	Select strategies for completing tasks	Deciphering and implementing a code
Attention	Focus selected attention on something over time	Underline specific numbers that appear in a long list of numbers
Simultaneous	See patterns from interrelated components	Remembering positions of a figure
Successive	Using materials presented in a specific order	Repeating a series of numbers in a correct order

Source: Adapted from Naglieri, 2005, and Naglieri and Das, 2005.

pieces are synthesized together much as one might appreciate a painting all at once. Successive processing is interpreting each piece of individual infomation separately, in sequential fashion. The third functional unit is responsible for planning and programming behavior. It is this last ability, planning, which has been hypothesized to be related to creativity (Naglieri & Kaufman, 2001). (See Table 6.3.)

Runco (2007) offers an interesting, alternative view. He argues that traditional investigations of the creativity-intelligence relationship may be ignoring the presence of heteroscedasticity—the idea that levels of creativity may vary considerably at different levels of intelligence. Acknowledging that a minimal level of intelligence is probably necessary for optimal creative contributions, Runco notes research (e.g., Hollingworth, 1942) suggesting that people with extremely high IQs often exhibit low levels of creativity.

Threshold Theory: How Much is Enough?

An interesting wrinkle in this topic is provided by the *threshold theory* (which Sternberg places in the overlapping sets category). Most studies that look at creativity and intelligence use divergent thinking tests (such as the TTCT) to measure creativity. They have generally found that creativity is significantly associated with psychometric measures of intelligence (especially verbally oriented measures). However, this relationship is not a particularly strong one (see Barron & Harrington, 1981; Kim, 2005). Creativity's correlation with IQ is maintained up to a certain level of performance on a traditional individual intelligence test. Traditional research has argued for a *threshold theory,* in which creativity and intelligence are positively, if moderately, correlated up until an IQ of approximately 120; in people with higher IQs, the two constructs show little relationship (e.g., Fuchs-Beauchamp, Karnes, & Johnson, 1993; Getzels & Jackson, 1962). More recently, however, the threshold theory has come under fire. Preckel, Holling, and Weise (2006) looked at measures of fluid intelligence and divergent thinking tests and found modest correlations across all levels of intellectual abilities. Kim (2005), in a meta-analysis of 21 studies, found virtually no support for the threshold theory, with very small positive correlations found between measures of ability and measures of creativity and divergent thinking.

It is notable, however, that nearly all of these studies do not use traditional, individually administered intelligence tests but rather rely on group tests. In addition, many of the studies in Kim's (2005) meta-analysis were more than 30 years old and therefore were conducted using intelligence tests that do not reflect current theory. One of the few research studies to use an individually administered, modern intelligence test was Sligh, Conners, and Roskos-Ewoldsen (2005), who used the Kaufman Adolescent and Adult Intelligence Scale (Kaufman & Kaufman, 1993). Sligh et al. delved deeper into the intelligence-creativity relationship by specifically examining the relationship between Gf and Gc and a measure of actual creative innovation. Gc showed the same moderate and positive relationship to creativity as past studies mentioned earlier; the relationship between crystallized intelligence and creativity increased up to a certain level of intelligence. In contrast, fluid intelligence showed the *opposite* pattern. People with lower levels of fluid intelligence did not show a strong relationship between their creativity and intelligence, but people with high levels of fluid intelligence did demonstrate a strong relationship. This finding implies that students who receive high *Gf* scores may be more likely to be creative than students who receive high *Gc* scores.

The Sligh et al. study also addresses a second major weakness in this line of research: the over-reliance on divergent thinking measures as the sole assessment of creativity. Few studies have been conducted that include measures of creative personality, creative products, and creative processes (other than divergent thinking). Given the distinct characteristics of assessments in these areas, highlighted throughout this book, the threshold theory may be best viewed as largely untested.

But given the existing studies, what do all of these results mean? Few studies contradict the idea that creative people tend to be fairly smart, and smart people are usually somewhat creative. But some of the tested-and-true ideas about the specific relationship are still unclear. If the threshold theory is correct, then there may be a certain point at which being smart stops helping creativity; recent psychometric studies, however, call the existence of the threshold effect into question.

Conclusion and Recommendations

Each of the five possible relationships in Sternberg's framework enjoys at least some empirical support (Sternberg & O'Hara, 1999), but the difficulty in interpreting empirical results illustrates the problems associated with reaching a consensus on the validity of any of these five relations (see Hattie & Rogers, 1986). For example, Haensly and Reynolds (1989) believe that Mednick's (1962) Association Theory supports the creativity as a subset of intelligence position, yet Sternberg and O'Hara (1999) feel that this body of work supports the overlapping sets position. In another example, if Gardner's work with creativity had come before his work with MI Theory, we would be tempted to argue that his efforts fall within the intelligence as a subset of creativity category. Extending this point further, Plucker and Lim (in press) have recently suggested that, when studying implicit theories of intelligence and creativity, more than one relationship may be pertinent in a given context.

Our view is that the complexity of possible intelligence-creativity relationships is not surprising. Whenever one compares two constructs, the way in which each construct is conceptualized and assessed will have a significant impact on any empirical results. In general, researchers and theorists clearly believe that intelligence and creativity are related. The exact way in which they are related is still very much in question. (See Rapid Reference 6.1.)

≡ Rapid Reference 6.1

How Can Intelligence and Creativity be Related?

Sternberg outlined five ways that intelligence and creativity may be related:

- Creativity may be a subset of intelligence (e.g., Guilford's SOI; the Cattell-Horn-Carroll theory)
- Intelligence may be a subset of creativity (e.g., Sternberg and Lubart's Investment Theory of Creativity; Amabile's Componential Theory of Creativity
- Creativity and intelligence may be overlapping sets (i.e., Renzulli's three-ring conception of giftedness; the PASS (Planning, Attention, Simultaneous, and Successive) theory)
- Creativity and intelligence may be coincident sets (i.e., they could be the same thing)
- Creativity and intelligence may be disjoint sets (i.e., they might have no relationship—no overlap—whatsoever)

LEARNING DISABILITIES AND CREATIVITY

One growing area of research related to intelligence and creativity is the possibility of measuring creativity in individuals with learning disabilities. Such measures may also help identify hidden strengths that may be able to be utilized in the classroom or workplace. There are many remedial treatments and programs that incorporate creative therapy for people with mental retardation or learning disabilities (e.g., Dossick & Shea, 1995), but there has been much less structured and empirical work investigating creativity in these populations.

One study of elementary school students found that those with learning disabilities engaged in less task persistence than average children and, as a result, scored lower on the TTCT in elaboration. On the other three components of the TTCT, however, the students with learning disabilities scored as well as the group of average children (Argulewicz, Mealor, & Richmond, 1979). Another study of gifted children with and without learning disabilities found that there were no significant differences between the two groups on measures of verbal creativity (Woodrum & Savage, 1994). A study of learning disabled children in self-contained classrooms used a naming task (in which students are asked to name things to eat). In this task, the children with learning disabilities were found to produce more original responses than a matched group of children with average abilities (Kaufman & Kaufman, 1980).

Cox and Cotgreave (1996) examined human figure drawings by 10-year-old children with mild learning disabilities (MLD) and 6- and 10-year-old children without MLD. They found that the drawings by the MLD children were easily distinguished from the other 10-year-olds, but not from the group of 6-year-old children, implying that while the MLD children may be developing artistic and creative abilities at a slower rate, the development still approaches a normal pattern.

Measures of creativity could particularly lend insight to individuals with dyslexia. LaFrance (1997), for example, points to creative thinking as being a particularly good way of distinguishing gifted students who have dyslexia, while Burrows and Wolf (1983) suggest creativity as a way of reducing frustration and improving self-attitudes in dyslexic children. The importance of creativity is consistent with other findings that show that dyslexic children frequently excel at divergent thinking (Vail, 1990). It is also interesting to note that case studies have been noted of individuals with dyslexia who were very creative in the literary domain—the very area of their learning disability (Rack, 1981).

Another learning disability with a strong connection to creativity is attention-deficit hyperactivity disorder (ADHD). Several scholars have proposed that the behaviors and characteristics associated with ADHD are highly similar to creative behaviors (Cramond, 1994; Leroux & Levitt-Perlman, 2000). Such traits as sensation and stimulation seeking and high usage of imagery, for example, are associated with both children with ADHD and highly creative children (Shaw, 1992). High IQ children with ADHD scored higher on tests of figural creativity than high IQ children who did not have ADHD (Shaw & Brown, 1990, 1991). Students with ADHD showed specific creativity strengths in fluency, originality, and elaboration on the TTCT (Gollmar, 2001).

Indeed, a study of undergraduates found that having a wider breadth of attention was correlated with writing poems that were judged to be more creative, and distracting noise disrupted creative performance more in those students with a wide breadth of attention (Kasof, 1997). In other words, the same aspects of ADHD that may make students more prone to be creative may also may them more prone to being distracted and, in some situations, producing lower quality work.

Creativity can even be analyzed with students with much more severe disabilities. Children with autism and Asperger's syndrome were able to generate changes to an object as part of the TTCT. These children made fewer changes than a sample of children without impairment, and their changes were more reality-based than imagination-based (Craig

& Baron-Cohen, 1999). But the very fact that creativity assessment was able to add information about this population's abilities is encouraging. An additional study compared children with autism and children with Asperger's syndrome (Craig & Baron-Cohen, 2000). They found that while both groups showed less imaginative events in a story-telling exercise than children without impairment, children with Asperger's syndrome were better able to demonstrate imagination than children with autism. This finding was also demonstrated with a drawing task (Craig, Baron-Cohen, & Scott, 2001).

In a related fashion, researchers studied human figure drawings in children with Down syndrome (Cox & Maynard, 1998). While Down syndrome children scored lower than both age mates and younger children, it is interesting to note that their drawings did not differ when drawn from a model or drawn from imagination, whereas both groups of non-Down syndrome children improved when drawn from a model. This finding may indicate that creative processes may be a comparative strength for children with Down syndrome.

One particular learning disability, Williams Syndrome (WS), is caused by a lack of genetic material that produces the protein elastin. Children with WS are developmentally delayed and often have profound disabilities in spatial cognition (Bellugi, Lichtenberger, Jones, Lai, & St. George, 2000). Yet children with WS have exceptional narrative skills for their cognitive ability level. Although their syntax was simpler and they were more likely to make errors in morphology than average children, they also used more evaluative devices and—of most interest for creativity studies—used much more elaboration in their narratives (Losh, Bellugi, Reilly, & Anderson, 2000). Between these narrative skills and the hypersociability associated with WS, these children often engage in storytelling (Jones et al., 2000). And while their stories use less complex syntax compared to average children, they are much *more* complex (and more expressive) than children with similar cognitive abilities with Down syndrome (Reilly, Klima, & Bellugi, 1990).

GIFTEDNESS AND CREATIVITY

The relationship between creativity and giftedness has also received substantial attention. Indeed, there are few areas—if any—in psychology and education where creativity assessment has been more frequently used than gifted education. Nearly every gifted education program has a formal assessment procedure to identify potential participants, and creativity assessments are often included in the battery of measures included in these identification systems.

For example, in a study of school districts' gifted identification systems, Callahan et al. (1995) found that creativity was frequently included in district definitions of giftedness, but that the measurement of creativity was fraught with problems (more about that later). In this section, we describe the major theories of giftedness—with an emphasis on their inclusion of creativity, review research on how schools' assess creativity within gifted identification systems, and provide a few recommendations for improving these systems are they relate to creativity.

Conceptions of Giftedness: Trickier than They First Appear

The constructs of *giftedness* and *talent* are often defined imprecisely, especially when compared to definitions of constructs such as mental retardation (Robinson, Zigler, & Gallagher, 2000). Robinson et al. note the difficulty in studying constructs that do not have readily agreed upon definitions such as those discussed in the *Diagnostic and Statistical Manual of Mental Disorders* (*DSM-IV-TR;* American Psychiatric Association, 2000) or codified in federal and state legislation. In addition, the prospect of arriving at a consensus definition becomes unlikely given the similar lack of precision surrounding related constructs such as creativity, intelligence, and leadership (Johnsen, 1997).

This conceptual fuzziness is reflected in practice: State legislation on gifted and talented education exists in 49 of 50 states, but the policies are inconsistent in terms of definition and level of detail (Passow & Rudnitski, 1993). As a result, these state definitions have led to rather poor identification procedures at the local, school level (Johnsen, 1997). The courts have been of little assistance, as

CAUTION

Each state has its own, often fuzzy, definition of giftedness. There is no uniform definition across the country or around the world.

the case law on gifted education is similarly muddied. This is probably due in part to a lack of understanding on the part of judges and juries about what giftedness and gifted education actually represent (Plucker, in press). The most recent federal report proposes a purposefully ambiguous definition of excellence and talent, further muddying the waters (OERI, 1993). Not surprisingly, this lack of a standard definition and the breadth of talents available have led to the existence of many theories and definitions of giftedness (see Gagné, 1993; Mönks & Mason, 1993; Sternberg & Davidson, 1986).

Part of the issue is that an unlimited breadth and depth of potential talents exist, and talents can emerge at different developmental levels (Passow, 1979; Robinson et al., 2000). But the inherent difficulty in defining giftedness cannot be an excuse for not attempting to define it: Schools seeking to promote academic excellence need to define what they are attempting to enhance, and state legislation is generally most effective when it can accurately define what it is addressing.

Although several authors have proposed complex organizations of theories, including those proposed by Sternberg and Davidson (1986; explicit: domain-specific, explicit: cognitive, explicit: developmental, implicit: theoretical) and Mönks and Mason (1993; trait-oriented, cognitive component, achievement-oriented, socio-cultural/psychosocial oriented), for the purposes of this discussion we propose a simpler, more pragmatic schema with two categories: early conceptions and contemporary approaches.

Early Conceptions: The Unitary Model

Traditional conceptions of giftedness emerged from theories of intelligence during the early part of the previous century. These views of intelligence, ranging from monocentric and related approaches (Cattell, 1987; Spearman, 1904) to differentiated models (Carroll, 1993; Guilford, 1967; Thurstone, 1938), viewed intelligence as a personal construct that resided within the individual. Although many of these theories acknowledge the role of the environment in the development of intelligence, the focus is firmly placed on the individual as the locus of control and unit of interest. Theories and models of creativity from this time similarly accented the individual (e.g., Guilford, 1950; Kris, 1952; MacKinnon, 1965).

Early conceptions of giftedness mirrored this emphasis on the individual (e.g., Hollingworth, 1942), and approaches to talent development based on these traditional conceptions of intelligence remain popular. For example, the Talent Search model initiated at Johns Hopkins University now works with more than 250,000 children per year (at varying levels of service) at several university-based regional centers across the country (Stanley, 1980; Stanley & Benbow, 1981). Many school districts around the country base their gifted education and talent development programs on the identification of high-ability children using instruments focused primarily on each individual's capabilities; in their national study, Callahan et al. (1995) found that 11 percent of the surveyed districts relied on a strict IQ definition of giftedness, making it the second most common definition.[2]

---

2. Robinson (2005) provides a strong, detailed defense of such psychometric approaches, which tend toward the unitary conceptions, although her analysis shows how such approaches can effectively deviate from strict "you're as gifted as your total IQ score" identification systems.

The Marland Definition

The federal government proposed a multifaceted definition of giftedness in the early 1970s that appears to have been based on the person-specific view of giftedness. This definition suggested that giftedness and talent are manifest in six areas: general intellectual ability, specific academic aptitude, creative or productive thinking, leadership ability, visual and performing arts, and psychomotor ability (Marland, 1972). The Marland definition has been extremely influential and is still used by many school districts in their identification of talented students. In the NRC/GT study, Callahan et al. (1995) found that nearly 50 percent of districts based their gifted education identification procedures on this definition, making it far and away the most popular definition in this setting.

Callahan et al. also uncovered interesting results regarding how districts assessed the "creative or productive thinking" aspects of the Marland definition (see also Hunsaker & Callahan, 1995). The most common measure used in assessing creativity was the SRBCSS, followed by the Structure of Intellect test and TTCT-Figural. The use of the SRBCSS is not surprising given its ease of use and ability to bring different perspectives into identification decisions, and the use of the TTCT is to be expected given its status as the most popular creativity assessment. The SOI test was mildly surprising, given that only one of the more than 400 districts relied on the SOI model as a definition of giftedness. But most surprising—if not shocking—was the fact that several districts reported using group-administered intelligence or achievement tests to assess students' creativity.[3] (See Rapid Reference 6.2.)

---

3. Districts reported using tests such as the California Achievement Test, Cognitive Abilities Test, Iowa Test of Basic Skills, Slosson Intelligence Test, and Stanford Achievement Test, among others. One district even reported using results from a group-administered academic achievement test to identify students with painting and drawing ability. That made us scratch our heads!

Rapid Reference 6.2

Marland Definition of Giftedness

The Marland definition of giftedness encompasses:
- general intellectual ability
- specific academic aptitude
- creative or productive thinking
- leadership ability
- abilities in the visual and performing arts
- psychomotor ability

Contemporary Approaches: The Case for Broadened Conceptions

Contemporary approaches to intelligence and creativity, such as Sternberg's (1985) triarchic theory, include explicit mechanisms with which the individual interacts with the environment. Others address these issues in a similar if more implicit manner, such as Ceci's (1990) bioecological approach and Gardner's (1983) theory of multiple intelligences. Perhaps the most well-known theory of giftedness, Renzulli's (1978, 1999) three-ring conception, focuses on the interaction among above average ability, creativity, and task commitment, within the context of personality, environmental, and affective factors.

Educational approaches to talent development based on these broader theories include Renzulli and Reis' (1985) Schoolwide Enrichment Model and several of the strategies described by Coleman and Cross (2001) and Karnes and Bean (2001). Recent alternative definitions of giftedness and talent (Feldhusen, 1998; OERI, 1993) are similar in spirit to Renzulli's three-ring conception and related programming models with their shared emphasis on a broadened conception and acknowledgement of multiple influences on the development of talent (i.e., systems views).

In most of these broader conceptions, creativity is either implicitly or explicitly included. Renzulli, as mentioned earlier, includes creativity in his three-ring conception, and Runco (2005) has defined creative giftedness as "(a) an exceptional level of interpretive capacity; (b) the discretion to use that capacity to construct meaningful and original ideas, options, and solution; and (c) the motivation to apply, maintain, and develop the interpretive capacity and discretion" (p. 303). In other words, both Runco and Renzulli appear to believe that creativity is a necessary but not sufficient component of giftedness, which reflects the general thinking in most differentiated theories of giftedness.

In the next section, we provide a more detailed analysis of three major conceptions of giftedness in order to provide some examples of how major thinkers view the creativity-giftedness relationship.

The Differentiated Model of Giftedness and Talent

One of the more pragmatic models for understanding the relationship between gifts and talents was proposed by Gagné (1993, 2000): the Differentiated Model of Giftedness and Talent (DMGT). The DMGT conceptualizes "gifts" as the innate abilities (or aptitudes) in at least one domain area (intellectual, creative, socioaffective, and sensorimotor) that place the individual in the top 10 percent of age peers (Gagné, 2000). Talent, on the other hand, is the demonstrated mastery of the gift as evidence by skills in academics, arts, business, leisure, social action, sports, or technology that place the individual in the top 10 percent of age peers. In short, "gifts" are the potential, and "talent" is the outcome.

It is possible for one to be identified as gifted (i.e., having the natural ability to excel) but never actually to manifest talent (i.e., underachievement). The reverse is not true however; for one to be identified as talented, one must first be gifted (Gagné, 2000). Thus, the process of transforming gifts into talent is commonly referred to as talent development. According to Gagné, talent development involves the systematic learning and practice needed for skills to be maximized, with higher order skills requiring more intense and long-term development.

Gifts alone do not account for all the variance in talent development.

This process is mediated by intrapersonal and environmental catalysts, which can either support or hinder the development of talent (Gagné, 2000). Intrapersonal catalysts include both physical (e.g., handicaps, health) and psychological characteristics (motivation, volition, self-management, and personality). Environmental catalysts include the milieu (i.e., the physical, cultural, familial, and social influences), persons (e.g., parents, teachers, peers, mentor), and provisions (e.g., programs, activities, and services), and events (e.g., encounters, awards, and accidents). It is also important to note that chance does play a role in genetic endowment, as well as in talent development, for example being born into a family and community that is willing and able to support (including emotionally and at times financially) the development of skills (Gagné, 2000).

Creativity is specifically mentioned as one of four aptitude domains, along with intellectual, socioaffective, and sensorimotor. Gagné refers to these four areas as natural abilities but does not provide a detailed model of what the creativity aptitude domain looks like, other than to note that it includes inventiveness, imagination, originality, and retrieval fluency.[4]

The Three-Ring Conception

The focus of Renzulli's work has been the creation of educational systems that help young people develop the skills, habits, and affect necessary for real-world creative productivity. Renzulli's (1978, 2005) Three-Ring Conception views giftedness as emerging from the interaction of well above-average ability, creativity, and task commitment, with each characteristic playing a critical role in the development of

---

4. To Gagné's credit, he notes that "many competing classification systems exist" for each of the four domains of natural talent and does not appear to prefer one over any other for the purposes of his model (2005, p. 101).

gifted behavior. Renzulli and his colleagues have conducted a number of studies of the validity of the Three-Ring Conception (e.g., Delisle & Renzulli, 1982; Renzulli, 1984, 1988), including studies of the effectiveness of educational interventions on which the model is based. The theory remains among the most popular conceptions of gifted-

> **DON'T FORGET**
>
> Renzulli's Three-Ring Conception views giftedness as emerging from the interaction of well above-average ability, creativity, and task commitment. The theory remains among the most popular conceptions of giftedness in the literature and in school districts

ness in the literature and in school districts (Callahan et al., 1995).

This theory is based upon studies of talented, successful adults (Renzulli, 1978, 1999) and—although not without its critics (e.g., Johnsen, 1999; Kitano, 1999; Olszewski-Kubilius, 1999)—benefits from its inclusion of multiple interacting factors and the broadening of criteria used in selection of gifted students. In addition, Renzulli emphasized the need to develop creative productive skills in addition to knowledge acquisition and presented evidence that his broadened identification procedures do indeed reduce inequalities such as a disproportionate representation of minorities in gifted education programs and gender equity (Renzulli, 1999). Perhaps the major contribution of the Three-Ring Conception—and the many related educational interventions which emerged from this model—is that it helped destroy the widely held belief that creativity was innate and could not be increased.

The Theory of Multiple Intelligences

Gardner's Theory of Multiple Intelligences (MI Theory; 1983, 1993; 1999) was a major milestone in encouraging educators to adopt broader definitions of human intelligence. He defined intelligence as "an ability or set of abilities that permit an individual to solve problems or fashion products that are of consequence in a particular cultural setting" (Ramos-Ford & Gardner, 1997, p.55), which—as noted in our discussion of intelligence—has obvious implications for conceptualizations of creativity. He conducted an extensive review of the literature and defined eight separate intelligences: linguistic (used when writing a novel), logical-mathematical (used when solving a mathematical problem), spatial (used when mentally rotating objects), musical (used in performing or composing music), bodily-kinesthetic (used in dancing or playing sports), interpersonal (used in understanding and interacting with other people), intrapersonal (used in understanding oneself), and naturalist (used in discerning patterns in nature). Additional intelligences are currently being considered, such as spiritual and existential intelligence, although Gardner has suggested that existential intelligence does not exist (Gardner, 1999).

MI theory offers an important framework for considering creative development and achievement. In fact, Gardner used his MI theory to examine the relationship between early giftedness and the later achievement of highly creative individuals (Gardner, 1993). Moreover, MI theory represents an important conceptual shift in expanding what might be considered intelligent behavior and, in turn, has the possibility to broaden the representations of creative giftedness. It does so by addressing a key debate amongst creativity scholars, specifically the general-domain specificity question in creativity research (see Kaufman & Baer, 2005; Sternberg, Grigorenko, & Singer, 2004). The domain debate centers on the question of whether creativity is domain-general or domain-specific.

Although MI Theory's popularity peaked after the Callahan et al. study (1995) was conducted, anecdotal evidence suggests that the theory was enormously influential in changing educator conceptions of intelligence, creativity, and talent. However, assessment within applied and educational settings has proven to be complex and fraught with difficulties, potentially limiting its impact on the identification of creativity within gifted identification systems (e.g., see Gardner, 1995; Plucker, 2000; Plucker, Callahan, & Tomchin, 1996; Pyryt, 2000). That said, and in a similar vein to our comment about Renzulli's larger impact on education, Gardner's work has indisputably helped broaden our conception of what talent and giftedness can be—and where it can be found.

> **DON'T FORGET**
> ....
> Gardner's Theory of Multiple Intelligences has encouraged educators to adopt broader and more domain-specific views of both creativity and intelligence. He has specified eight separate intelligences: linguistic, logical-mathematical, spatial, musical, bodily-kinesthetic, interpersonal, intrapersonal, and naturalist.

Conclusion and Recommendations

Gifted identification systems are, for all practical intents and purposes, the main application of creativity assessments in the United States, and they also serve as a great laboratory for the development, evaluation, and refinement of such measures. And, as gifted education grows in popularity around the world, the opportunities for the development and use of cutting-edge creativity assessments are enormous.

However, research on how creativity is conceptualized and measured in gifted education systems is not encouraging. Although this research is becoming dated, there is little anecdotal evidence that the situation is changing. With this in mind, we encourage educators and psychologists to follow the guidelines for multi-faceted and flexible identification procedures provided by Johnsen (2008), Renzulli and Reis (1985), and others. This at least allows creativity in the door, as the use of single criterion systems and their traditional focus on intelligence obviously precludes much consideration of creativity.

In a similar vein, when assessing creativity as part of a gifted identification system, special care should be devoted to matching the definition of creativity with the assessment being used. This avoids the stunning mismatch identified by Callahan et al. (1995) and Hunsaker and Callahan (1995), where academic achievement tests are used to identify creativity. But doing so also avoids the less obvious problem of, for example, using the TTCT to identify creative students when the school's definition of creativity has little to do with divergent thinking (for example, a school that might consider hands-on problem-solving creativity as most important).

But our major recommendation in this area is to encourage researchers to work with educators of the gifted to develop more robust and psychometrically sound gifted identification systems. These systems need to be easy to administer, yet highly reliable and conceptually valid. If not, educators will continue to fall back to group-administered intelligence and achievement tests as the primary—if not sole—criterion for identification as gifted.

🐗 TEST YOURSELF 🐗

1. **Most differentiated theories of giftedness, such as the theories of Runco and Renzulli, suggest that creativity is:**
    (a) the primary component of giftedness
    (b) only tangentially related to giftedness
    (c) completely unrelated to giftedness
    (d) a necessary but not sufficient component of giftedness

2. **Which of the following best describes what we know about the relationship between creativity and intelligence?**
    (a) There is no relationship whatsoever.
    (b) Creativity requires intelligence, so there is a clear and strong correlation between the two.
    (c) Intelligence requires creativity, so there is a clear and strong correlation between the two.
    (d) The research in this area is murky, which makes it hard to state the nature of the relationship clearly.

3. **Which learning disability is associated with strong narrative and storytelling skills?**

   (a) Down syndrome

   (b) Williams syndrome

   (c) Asperger's syndrome

   (d) Autism

4. **Renzulli's three-ring conception of giftedness, which theorizes that giftedness is caused by the confluence of high intellectual ability, creativity, and task commitment, is an example of a theory that suggests the relationship between creativity and intelligence is:**

   (a) one of over-lapping but distinct sets

   (b) one in which creativity is subsumed under intelligence

   (c) one in which intelligence is subsumed under creativity

   (d) one in which there is no relationship between intelligence and creativity

5. **One place where creativity assessment has been very widely used is in:**

   (a) screening applicants for jobs

   (b) gifted and talented programs

   (c) special education

   (d) validation of intelligence tests

6. **Which of the following is NOT conceptualized as part of giftedness, according to the Marland definition?**

   (a) general intellectual ability

   (b) attitudes toward school

   (c) creative or productive thinking

   (d) specific academic aptitude

(continued)

7. **Divergent production, which is believed by many to be an important part of creativity, was one of five cognitive operations that underlies intelligence, by which of the following theorists?**

   (a) Amabile

   (b) Cattell

   (c) Gardner

   (d) Guilford

8. **Gardner's Multiple Intelligence Model suggests there are at least eight different domains or intelligences. This has influenced educators' conceptions of:**

   (a) intelligence only

   (b) creativity only

   (c) both intelligence and creativity

   (d) neither intelligence nor creativity

9. **The need to match the definition of creativity with the assessment being used implies which of the following?**

   (a) Academic achievement tests should not be employed as measures of creativity.

   (b) Divergent thinking tests such as the TTCT should not be used to identify creative students when the school's definition of creativity has little to do with divergent thinking.

   (c) Educators and psychologists should employ multi-faceted and flexible identification procedures.

   (d) All of the above.

Answers: 1. d; 2. d; 3. b; 4. a; 5. b; 6. b; 7. d; 8. c; 9. d.

Seven

MOVING FORWARD

What kinds of creative assessment might we expect, or hope for, in the future? We can't say for sure, of course, but we believe that the ideal creativity assessment would be one based on a hierarchical mode of creativity, one that posits both domain-general and domain-specific elements. The issue of domain specificity versus domain generality—that is, the question of whether the skills and traits that lead to creative performance in each domain are different or the same across domains—is one of the major unresolved issues in creativity research. The answer to that question will influence the kinds of creativity assessment that will be most valid. As with many controversies of this kind, the truth is likely to lie somewhere in between the two extreme positions.[1] One such model is the hierarchical Amusement Park Theoretical (APT) Model of creativity, which posits both general factors that impact creativity in all areas and several levels of domain-specific factors that impact creative performance in increasingly narrow ranges of activities (Baer & Kaufman, 2005; Kaufman & Baer, 2004, 2005). Another theory, proposed by Plucker and Beghetto (2004), argues that creativity has both specific

---

1. As already noted in Chapter 1, two of this book's authors took opposing views on this issue in the only Point-Counterpoint pair of articles ever published in the *Creativity Research Journal* (Baer, 1998; Plucker, 1998).

and general components, with that the level of specificity-generality changing with the social context and as one develops through childhood into adulthood.

If such models were used to guide the creation of a collection of creativity assessment devices, it might include both domain-general assessments and domain-specific assessments. Which domain would be selected? Based on a factor analysis of responses to a survey of 3,553 people, each of whom self-reported their creativity in the 56 domains of the Creativity Domain Questionnaire, Kaufman, Cole and Baer (in press) proposed general thematic areas: artistic-verbal, artistic-visual, entrepreneur, interpersonal, math/science, performance, and problem-solving creativity. This structure is only one of many possibilities; consider Feist's seven "domains of mind" (psychology, physics, biology, linguistics, math, art, and music), or Gardner's multiple intelligences, discussed earlier in Chapter Six.

A complete creativity assessment package might include assessment devices that tap creativity in each of these domains, and these might also be used to generate an overall creativity score.

What would those assessments look like? They might include both divergent-thinking tests that focus on each particular general thematic area and performance assessments that tap creativity on tasks in each domain, scored using the Consensual Assessment Technique. Or perhaps creativity researchers and test developers will find shorter, easier-to-score alternatives to the very resource-intensive Consensual Assessment Technique.

Another possibility would be to apply the ideas of "intelligent testing" to creativity assessment. This concept is a popular philosophy of IQ testing that disdains global scores and has had a tremendous influence on the field (Kaufman, 1979, 1994). Using this system, the tester is elevated above the test. The global scores mean little by themselves. The key is interpreting the scores in context. The persons administering the test are expected to use their qualifications and training and bring their own experience to the testing session. In this manner, the tester can help the child or adult being tested by understanding and interpreting a wide range of behaviors, making inferences about any observed problem-solving strategies, and applying the latest theories and research results directly to the person's specific set of scores. Every aspect of psychology is brought into play to interpret a profile of scores in the context of accumulated research, theory, and clinical practice. This profile is used to help solve problems and create solutions for the person tested— i.e., providing answers to the referral questions—not merely as a label or classification system (Kaufman, 1979, 1994).

We believe that this approach can be applied to creativity research (Kaufman & Baer, 2006). A qualified tester would be well versed in the fields of social, cognitive, and educational psychology (among others). The pattern of scores in the different domains could be interpreted for its comparative strengths and weaknesses. Rather than merely producing a single number that is of little use to a student, this new domain-specific creativity could help students discover and validate areas of creative talent in themselves. In addition, an administrator using the "intelligent testing" approach could look for signs of insufficient motivation, a thinking style that might conflict with the task, or other additional areas that could be improved for enhanced creative potential.

This concept, we believe, would be in line with Torrance's original aims in the development of the TTCT (Torrance, 1966, 1974). Torrance did not necessarily design his tests for the use to which they are most commonly put these days—identification of students for gifted/talented programs (Kim, 2006). His primary goals in developing these tests were to help us better understand the human mind and its functioning; to find ways to better individualize instruction, including remedial and psychotherapeutic interventions; to evaluate the effectiveness of educational programs; and to become more sensitive to latent potential in individuals.

TAKE HOME POINTS

We will now present a table with a brief overview of the types of assessments we have covered, including both advantages and disadvantages (see Table 7.1).

With all of these caveats and lack of resolution over one "perfect" measure, why would anyone want to include a measure of creativity in their battery of assessments? There is certainly cause to hesitate: Many creativity tests have mixed or poor evidence of validity. We would also not necessarily recommend the routine use of creativity tests in every assessment. We believe there are many compelling reasons and situations where using a measure of creativity could greatly benefit an overall evaluation, however. For example, we advise the use of a creativity measure when:

Table 7.1 Major Ways of Assessing Creativity

Type of Assessment	Examples	Advantages	Disadvantages
Divergent Thinking Tests	Torrance Tests of Creative Thinking	Years of research results in a well-studied measure	May only tap into one aspect of creativity
Consensual Assessment Techniques	Having experts rate a creative product	Allows for very domain-specific information about creativity	Very time-consuming and expensive
Assessment by Others	Scales for Rating the Behavioral Characteristics of Superior Students or other checklists	Typically, creativity is rated by a teacher, peer, or parent who knows the individual	Many issues with validity/reliability; there may be unconscious biases
Self Assessment	Asking someone to rate his or her own creativity	Quick, cheap, and has high face validity	People are not always the best judge of their creativity

- You have reason to think that traditional IQ or achievement tests may not tap all of a person's potential. Divergent-thinking tests may help give a more comprehensive understanding of a person's overall abilities. The same can be said of creativity checklists completed by teachers.
- A test-taker is at risk for a stereotype threat reaction to traditional tests. Almost all measures of creativity show less ethnicity and gender biases than standard IQ and achievement tests.
- Parents, teachers, or peers describe an individual as being especially creative.
- A test-taker has a learning disability that may impact individual scores on a traditional ability or achievement measure.
- You are trying to assess creative abilities in a particular area, such as creative writing, artistic creativity, or musical creativity.
- Giving people a chance to show what they can do (using a real-world task such as writing a short story or making a collage, then judging their creations using the Consensual Assessment Technique) can help spotlight creative talent that might be overlooked in a traditional battery of assessments.
- You need to judge the creativity of a group of artifacts (poems, musical compositions, science fair projects, etc.) as part of a competition and you want to include (or focus on) creativity in your assessment. This is a perfect opportunity to use the Consensual Assessment Technique.
- You are selecting students for a gifted/talented program and want to follow national guidelines to use multiple selection criteria (rather than rely solely on IQ and achievement data). Most creativity measures, although not necessarily the only solution for such selections, may serve as part of a broader evaluation that can add to the overall picture of each candidate.

It is important to reiterate that we do *not* support administering a creativity test instead of a traditional IQ, achievement, or behavior test. We believe that all of these measures can work together to create the fullest possible picture of an individual, much as cereal, toast, juice, and eggs may all comprise a healthy, nutritious breakfast.

FINAL THOUGHTS

Creativity has many facets, appears in many guises, and is understood (and assessed) in many ways. Almost two centuries ago, in his "The American Scholar" oration, Ralph Waldo Emerson (1937/1998) noted that:

> There are creative manners, there are creative actions, and creative words; manners, actions, words, that is, indicative of no custom or authority, but springing spontaneous from the mind's own sense of good and fair. (p. 4)

Emerson mentions just three kinds of creativity here (he adds others later in his talk), but even these three suggest the complexity of creativity. There is perhaps no upper limit to the kinds of creativity one could posit: the above-mentioned Creativity Domain Questionnaire (Kaufman, Cole, & Baer, in press) assesses 56 domains, and the Creativity Achievement Questionnaire (Carson, Peterson, & Higgins, 2005) offers 96 items, but in both cases these many varieties of creativity were winnowed from still much longer lists in the interest of presenting questionnaires that could be completed in a reasonable period of time. With so many kinds of creativity to assess, is it any wonder that creativity assessment is both complex and difficult?

Our goal has been to describe the myriad ways that creativity is assessed and to explain how and when they might appropriately be used (as well as what cautions are in order when employing each of these techniques). Creativity assessment is a work in progress—we know far less about creativity and its measurement than we would like to know—but that is not to say that we know nothing at all. We hope that readers, armed with the tools we have described, will be able to find the most appropriate technique, or combination of techniques, for each of their particular creativity assessment purposes.

References

Agars, M. D., Kaufman, J. C., & Locke, T. R. (2008). Social influence and creativity in organizations: A multilevel lens for theory, research, and practice. To appear in M. Mumford, S. T. Hunter, and K. E. Bedell-Avers (Eds.), *Multi-level issues in organizational innovation* (Multi-level issues series) (pp. 3–62). Amsterdam, The Netherlands: JAI Press.

Alliger, G. M. (1988). Do zero correlations really exist among measures of different intellectual abilities? *Educational and Psychological Measurement, 48,* 275–280.

Allik, J., & McCrae, R. R. (2004). Toward a geography of personality traits: Patterns of profiles across 36 cultures. *Journal of Cross-Cultural Psychology, 35,* 13–28.

Amabile, T. M. (1982). Social psychology of creativity: A consensual assessment technique. *Journal of Personality and Social Psychology, 43,* 997–1013.

Amabile, T. M. (1983). *The social psychology of creativity.* New York: Springer Verlag.

Amabile, T. M. (1996). *Creativity in context: Update to "The Social Psychology of Creativity."* Boulder, CO: Westview Press.

Amabile, T. M., & Gryskiewicz, N. D. (1989). The creative environment scales: Work environment inventory. *Creativity Research Journal, 2,* 231–253.

Amabile, T. M., Phillips, E., and Collins, M. A. (1994). Person and Environment in Talent Development: The Case of Creativity. In *Talent Development: Proceedings of the 1993 Henry B. and Jocelyn Wallace National Research Symposium on Talent Development,* edited by N. Colangelo, S. G. Assouline and D. L. Ambroson. Unionville, N.Y.: Trillium Press.

American Psychiatric Association (2000). *Diagnostic and statistical manual of mental disorders* (4th ed., text revision). Washington, DC: Author.

Argulewicz, E. N (1985). Test review of Scales For Rating the Behavioral

Characteristics of Superior Students. From J. V. Mitchell, Jr. (Ed.), *The ninth mental measurements yearbook* [Electronic version]. Retrieved January 9, 2008, from the Buros Institute's *Test Reviews Online* website: http://www.unl.edu/buros

Argulewicz, E. N., Elliott, S. N., & Hall, R. (1982). Comparison of behavioral ratings of Anglo-American and Mexican-American gifted children. *Psychology in the Schools, 19,* 469–472.

Argulewicz, E. N., & Kush, J. C. (1984). Concurrent validity of the SRBCSS Creativity Scale for Anglo-American and Mexican-American gifted students. *Educational & Psychological Research, 4,* 81–89.

Argulewicz, E. N., Mealor, D. J., & Richmond, B. D. (1979). Creative abilities of learning disabled children. Journal of Learning Disabilities, 12, 21–24.

Arnold, K. D., & Subotnik, R. F. (1994). Lessons from contemporary longitudinal studies. In R. R. Subotnik & K. D. Arnold (Eds.), *Beyond Terman: Contemporary longitudinal studies of giftedness and talent* (pp. 437–451). Norwood, NJ: Ablex.

Aslan, A. E., & Puccio, G. J. (2006). Developing and testing a Turkish version of Torrance's tests of creative thinking: A study of adults. *Journal of Creative Behavior, 40,* 163–177.

Assessment Reform Network. (2002). What do the experts say about high-stakes testing? [Online]. Available: http://www.fairtest.org/arn/experts.html

Baer, J. (1993a). Creativity *and divergent thinking: A task-specific approach.* Hillsdale, NJ: Lawrence Erlbaum Associates.

Baer, J. (1993b, December/January). Why you shouldn't trust creativity tests. *Educational Leadership,* 80–83.

Baer, J. (1994a). Divergent thinking is not a general trait: A multi-domain training experiment. *Creativity Research Journal, 7,* 35–46.

Baer, J. (1994b). Performance assessments of creativity: Do they have long-term stability? *Roeper Review, 7*(1), 7–11.

Baer, J. (1994c). Why you *still* shouldn't trust creativity tests. *Educational Leadership, 52*(1), 72.

Baer, J. (1996). The effects of task-specific divergent-thinking training. *Journal of Creative Behavior, 30,* 183–187.

Baer, J. (1997). Gender differences in the effects of anticipated evaluation on creativity. *Creativity Research Journal, 10,* 25–31.

Baer, J. (1998a). The case for domain specificity in creativity. *Creativity Research Journal, 11,* 173–177.

Baer, J. (1998b). Gender differences in the effects of extrinsic motivation on creativity. *Journal of Creative Behavior, 32,* 18–37.

Baer, J. (2003). Impact of the Core Knowledge Curriculum on creativity. *Creativity Research Journal, 15,* 297–300.

Baer, J. (2005, August). *Gender and Creativity.* Paper presented at the annual meeting of the American Psychological Association, Washington, DC.

Baer, J., & Kaufman, J. C. (2005). Bridging Generality and Specificity: The Amusement Park Theoretical (APT) Model of Creativity. *Roeper Review, 27,* 158–163.

Baer, J., & Kaufman, J. C. (in press). Gender differences in creativity. *Journal of Creative Behavior.*

Baer, J., Kaufman, J. C., & Gentile, C. A. (2004). Extension of the consensual assessment technique to nonparallel creative products. *Creativity Research Journal, 16,* 113–117.

Baer, J., & McKool, S. (in press). Assessing creativity using the consensual assessment. In C. Schreiner (Ed.), *Handbook of Assessment technologies, methods, and applications in higher education.* Hershey, Pennsylvania: IGI Global.

Baer, M., & Oldham, G. R. (2006). The curvilinear relation between experienced creative time pressure and creativity: Moderating effects of Openness to Experience and support for creativity. *Journal of Applied Psychology, 91,* 963–970.

Bandura, A. (1997). *Self-efficacy: The exercise of control.* New York: Freeman.

Barron, F. (1969). *Creative person and creative process.* New York: Holt, Rinehart, & Winston.

Barron, F. (1988). Putting creativity to work. In R. J. Sternberg (Ed.), *The nature of creativity* (pp. 76–98). New York: Cambridge University Press.

Barron, F., & Harrington, D. M. (1981). Creativity, intelligence, and personality. *Annual Review of Psychology, 32,* 439–476.

Bartlett, T. (March 15, 2002). Undergraduates heed the writer's muse. *Chronicle of Higher Education,* A39–45.

Basadur, M. S., Wakabayashi, M., & Graen, G. B. (1990). Individual problem solving styles and attitudes toward divergent thinking before and after training. *Creativity Research Journal, 3,* 22–32.

Beghetto, R. A. (2006). Creative self-efficacy: Correlates in middle and secondary students. *Creativity Research Journal, 18,* 447–457.

Bellugi, U., Lichtenberger, E. O., Jones, W., Lai, Z., & St. George, M. (2000). The neurocognitive profile of Williams syndrome: A complex pattern of strengths and weaknesses. *Journal of Cognitive Neuroscience,* 12, 7–29.

Benet-Martínez, V., & Oishi, S. (in press). Culture and personality. In O. P. John, R. W. Robins, & L. A. Pervin (Eds.), *Handbook of personality: Theory and research.* New York: Guilford.

Besemer, S. P., & O'Quin, K. (1993). Assessing creative products: Progress and potentials. In S. G. Isaksen, M. C. Murdock, R. L. Firestien, & D. J. Treffinger (Eds.), Nurturing and developing creativity: The emergence of a discipline (pp. 331–349). Norwood, NJ: Ablex Publishing Company.

Blair, C. S., & Mumford, M. D. (2007). Errors in idea evaluation: Preference for the unoriginal? *Journal of Creative Behavior, 41,* 197–222.

Bowers, K. S., Regehr, G., Balthazard, C. G., & Parker, K. (1990). Intuition in the context of discovery. *Cognitive Psychology, 22,* 72–110.

Bracken, B. A., & Brown, E. F. (2006). Behavioral identification and assessment of gifted and talented students. *Journal of Psychoeducational Assessment, 24,* 112–122.

Burrows, D., & Wolf, B. (1983). Creativity and the dyslexic child: A classroom view. *Annals of Dyslexia, 33,* 269–274.

Callahan, C. M. (1991). The assessment of creativity. In N. Colangelo & G. A. Davis (Eds.), *Handbook of gifted education* (pp. 219–235). Boston: Allyn and Bacon.

Callahan, C. M., Hunsaker, S. L., Adams, C. M., Moore, S. D., & Bland, L. C. (1995). *Instruments used in the identification of gifted and talented students* (Report No. RM-95130). Charlottesville, VA: National Research Center on the Gifted and Talented.

Callahan, C. M., Tomlinson, C. A., Hunsaker, S. L., Bland, L. C., & Moon, T. (1995). *Instruments and evaluation designs used in gifted programs.* Storrs, CT: National Research Center on the Gifted and Talented.

Cameron, B. A., Brown, D. M., Carson, D. K., Meyer, S. S., & Bittner, M. T. (1993). Children's creative thinking and color discrimination. *Perceptual and Motor Skills, 76,* 595–598.

Carroll, J. B. (1993). *Human cognitive abilities: A survey of factor-analytic studies.* New York: Cambridge University Press.

Carson, S. (2006, April). *Creativity and Mental Illness.* Invitational Panel Discussion Hosted by Yale's Mind Matters Consortium, New Haven, CT.

Carson, S., Peterson, J. B. & Higgins, D. M. (2005). Reliability, validity and factor structure of the creative achievement questionnaire. *Creativity Research Journal, 17,* 37–50.

Cattell, R. B. (1987). *Intelligence: Its structure, growth and action.* Amsterdam: Elsevier.

Cattell, R. B., & Butcher, H. (1968). The *prediction of achievement and creativity.* Indianapolis, IN: Bobbs-Merrill.

Ceci, S. J. (1990). *On intelligence—more or less: A bio-ecological treatise on intellectual development.* Englewood Cliffs, NJ: Prentice Hall.

Center for Creative Learning. (2002a). *Review of the Creativity Assessment Packet.* Retrieved November 10, 2007, from the Center For Creative Learning website: http://www.creativelearning.com/Assess/test21.htm

Center for Creative Learning. (2002b). *Review of the Scales for Rating the Behavioral Characteristics of Superior Students.* Retrieved November 10, 2007, from the Center For Creative Learning website: http://www.creative learning.com/Assess/test55.htm

Center for Creative Learning. (2002c). *Review of the Meeker Creativity Rating*

Scale. Retrieved November 11, 2007, from the Center For Creative Learning website: http://www.creativelearning.com/Assess/test40.htm

Center for Creative Learning. (2002d). *Review of Gifted Evaluation Scale–Second Edition (GES-II).* Retrieved January 3, 2008, from the Center For Creative Learning website: http://www.creativelearning.com/Assess/test30.htm

Chamorro-Premuzic, T., Furnham, A., & Moutafi, J. (2004). The relationship between estimated and psychometric personality and intelligence scores. *Journal of Research in Personality, 38,* 505–513.

Chan, D. W. (2005). Self-perceived creativity, family hardiness, and emotional intelligence of Chinese gifted students in Hong Kong. *Journal of Secondary Gifted Education, 16,* 47–56.

Chan, D. W., Cheung, P.-C., Lau, S., Wu, W. Y. H., Kwong, J. M. L., & Li, W.-L. (2000–2001). Assessing ideational fluency in primary students in Hong Kong. *Creativity Research Journal, 13,* 359–365.

Chand, I., & Runco, M. A. (1993). Problem finding skills as components in the creative process. *Personality & Individual Differences, 14,* 155–162.

Charles, R. E., & Runco, M. A. (2000–2001). Developmental trends in the evaluative and divergent thinking of children. *Creativity Research Journal, 13,* 417–437.

Charyton, C., Jagacinski, R. J., Merrill, J. A., & Lilly, B. (in press). CEDA: A Research Instrument for Creative Engineering Design Assessment. *Psychology of Aesthetics and Creativity in the Arts.*

Chen, C., Kasof, J., Himsel, A. J., Greenberger, E., Dong, Q., & Xue, G. (2002). Creativity in drawings of geometric shapes: A cross-cultural examination with the consensual assessment technique. *Journal of Cross Cultural Psychology, 33,* 171–187.

Chen, C.-Y., & Michael, W. B. Higher-order abilities conceptualized within Guilford's Structure-of-Intellect (SOI) Model for a sample of United States Coast Guard Academy cadets: A reanalysis of an SOI data base. *Educational and Psychological Measurement, 53,* 941–950.

Chen Shyuefee, A., & Michael, W. B. (1993). First-order and

higher-order factors of creative social intelligence within Guilford's Structure-of-Intellect Model: A reanalysis of a Guilford data base. *Educational and Psychological Measurement, 53,* 619–641.

Chi, M. T. H. (1997). Creativity: Shifting across ontological categories flexibly. In T. B. Ward, S. M. Smith, & J. Vaid (Eds.), *Creative thought: An investigation of conceptual structures and processes* (pp. 209–234). Washington, DC: American Psychological Association.

Chrisler, J. C. (1991). The effect of premenstrual symptoms on creative thinking. In D. L. Taylor & N. F. Woods (Eds.), *Menstruation, health, and illness* (p. 73–83). New York: Hemisphere.

Chusmir, L. H., & Koberg, C. S. (1986). Creativity differences among managers. *Journal of Vocational Behavior, 29,* 240–253.

Clapham, M. M. (1996). The construct validity of divergent scores in the Structure-of-Intellect Learning Abilities Test. *Educational and Psychological Measurement, 56,* 287–292.

Clapham, M. M., Cowdery, E. M., King, K. E., & Montang, M. A. (2005). Predicting work activities with divergent thinking tests: A longitudinal study. *Journal of Creative Behavior, 39,* 149–167.

Clarizio, H. F., & Mehrens, W. A. (1985). Psychometric limitations of Guilford's Structure-of-Intellect model for identification and programming of the gifted. *Gifted Child Quarterly, 29,* 113–120.

Clark, P. M., & Mirels, H. L. (1970). Fluency as a pervasive element in the measurement of creativity. *Journal of Educational Measurement, 7,* 83–86.

Claxton, A. F., Pannells, T. C., & Rhoads, P. A. (2005). Developmental trends in the creativity of school-age children. *Creativity Research Journal, 17,* 327–335.

Coleman, L. J., & Cross, T. L. (2001). Being gifted in school: An introduction to education, guidance, and teaching: Book review. *Gifted Child Quarterly, 45,* 65–67.

Conti, R., Coon, H., & Amabile, T. M. (1996). Evidence to support the componential model of creativity: Secondary analyses of three studies. *Creativity Research Journal, 9,* 385–389.

Coffman, W. E. (1985). Review of Structure of Intellect Learning Abilities Test. In J. V. Mitchell, Jr. (Ed.), *The ninth mental measurements yearbook* (pp. 1486–1488). Lincoln, NE: Buros Institute of Mental Measurements.

Cooper, E. (1991). A critique of six measures for assessing creativity. *Journal of Creative Behavior, 25,* 194–204.

Costa, P. T., & McCrae, R. R. (1992). *Revised NEO Personality Inventory and NEO Five-Factor Inventory, Professional Manual.* Odessa, FL: Psychological Assessment Resources, Inc.

Cox, M. V., Koyasu, M., Hiranuma, H., & Perara, J. (2001). Children's human figure drawings in the UK and Japan; The effects of age, sex, and culture. *British Journal of Developmental Psychology, 19,* 275–292.

Cox, M. V., & Maynard, S. (1998). The human figure drawings of children with Down syndrome. *British Journal of Developmental Psychology, 16,* 133–137.

Cox, M. V., Perara, J., & Fan, X. (1998). Children's drawing ability in the UK and China. *Psychologia: An International Journal of Psychology in the Orient, 41,* 171–182.

Craig, J., & Baron-Cohen, S. (1999). Creativity and imagination in autism and Asperger syndrome. *Journal of Autism and Developmental Disorders, 29,* 319–326.

Craig, J., & Baron-Cohen, S. (2000). Story-telling ability in children with autism or Asperger syndrome: A window into the imagination. *Israel Journal of Psychiatry, 37,* 64–70.

Craig, J., Baron-Cohen, S. & Scott, F. (2001). Drawing ability in autism: A window into the imagination. *Israel Journal of Psychiatry, 38,* 242–253.

Cramond, B. (1993). The Torrance Tests of Creative Thinking: From design through establishment of predictive validity. In R. F. Subotnik & K. D. Arnold (Eds.), *Beyond Terman: Contemporary longitudinal studies of giftedness and talent* (pp. 229–254). Norwood, NJ: Ablex.

Cramond, B. (1994, October). We *can* trust creativity tests. *Educational Leadership,* 70–71.

Cropley, D. & Cropley, A. (2005). Engineering creativity: A systems concept of functional creativity. In J. C. Kaufman & J. Baer (Eds.), *Cre-*

ativity across domains: Faces of the muse (pp. 169–185). Mahwah, NJ: Lawrence Erlbaum Associates.

Csikszentmihalyi, M. (1996). *Creativity*. New York: HarperCollins.

Csikszentmihalyi, M. (1999). Implications of a systems perspective for the study of creativity. In R. J. Sternberg (Ed.), *Handbook of creativity* (pp. 313–335). Cambridge: Cambridge University Press.

Csikszentmihalyi, M., and Getzels, J. W. (1971). Discovery-oriented behavior and the originality of creative products: A study with artists. *Journal of Personality and Social Psychology, 19*, 47–52.

Cummings, J. A. (1989). Review of the Structure of Intellect Learning Abilities Test. In J. C. Conoley & J. J. Kramer (Eds.), *The tenth mental measurements yearbook*. Lincoln, NE: Buros Institute of Mental Measurements. (Retrieved on-line March 3, 2008).

Cunningham, C. H., Thompson, B., Ashton, H. L., & Wakefield, J. A. (1978). Use of SOI abilities for prediction. *Gifted Child Quarterly, 22,* 506–512.

Damarin, F. L. (1985). Test review of Creativity Assessment Packet. From J. V. Mitchell, Jr. (Ed.), *The ninth mental measurements yearbook* [Electronic version]. Retrieved January 9, 2008, from the Buros Institute's *Test Reviews Online* website: http://www.unl.edu/buros

Das, J. P., Naglieri, J. A., & Kirby, J. R. (1994). *Assessment of cognitive processes: The PASS theory of intelligence*. Boston: Allyn & Bacon.

Davidson, J. E., & Sternberg, R. J. (Eds.). (2003). *The psychology of problem solving*. New York: Cambridge University Press.

Delisle, J. R., & Renzulli, J. S. (1982). The Revolving Door Identification and Programming Model: Correlates of Creative Production. *Gifted Child Quarterly, 26,* 89–95.

De Sousa Filho, P.G., & Alencar, E. (2003). Creative thinking abilities in institutionalized and non-institutionalized children. *Estudos de Psicologia, 20*(3), 23–35.

Dollinger, S. J., Burke, P. A., & Gump, N. W. (2007). Creativity and values. *Creativity Research Journal, 19,* 91–104.

Dollinger, S. J., & Shafran, M. (2005). Note on Consensual Assessment

Technique in creativity research. *Perceptual and Motor Skills, 100*(3), 592–598.

Domino, G. (1974). Assessment of cinematographic creativity. *Journal of Personality and Social Psychology, 30,* 150–154.

Dominowski, R. L., & Dallob, P. (1995). Insight and problem solving. In R. J. Sternberg & J. E. Davidson (Eds.), *The nature of insight* (pp. 33–62). Cambridge, MA: The MIT Press.

Donnell, P. A. (2005). *The relationship between middle school gifted students' creativity test scores and self-perceptions regarding friendship, sensitivity, and divergent thinking variables.* Unpublished doctoral dissertation, Texas A&M University.

Dorfman, L., Locher, P., & Martindale, C. (Eds.). (2006). New Directions in Aesthetics, Creativity, and the Arts (Foundations and Frontiers in Aesthetics). Amityville, NY: Baywood Press.

Dossick, J., & Shea, E. (1995). *Creative: therapy III: 52 more exercises for groups.* Sarasota, FL: Professional Resource Press.

Dudek, S. Z., & Verreault, R. (1989). The creative thinking and ego functioning of children. *Creativity Research Journal, 2,* 64–86.

Dunning, D. A. (2005). *Self-insight: Roadblocks and detours on the path to knowing thyself.* New York: Psychology Press.

Dunning, D., Johnson, K., Ehrlinger, J., & Kruger, J. (2003). Why people fail to recognize their own incompetence. *Current Directions in Psychological Science, 12,* 83–86.

Eisenman, R. & Grove, M. S. (1972). Self-ratings of creativity, semantic differential ratings, and preferences for polygons varying in complexity, simplicity, and symmetry. *Journal of Psychology: Interdisciplinary and Applied, 81,* 63–67.

Emerson, R. W. (1837/1998). "The American Scholar." An oration delivered before the Phi Beta Kappa Society, at Cambridge, August 31, 1837, published in *Nature; Addresses and Lectures,* and retrieved December 18, 2007, from http://rwe.org/works/Nature_addresses_1_The_American_Scholar.htm

Enright, M. K., & Gitomer, D. H. (1989). Toward a Description of Successful Graduate Students (GRE Board Professional Rep. No. 89–09, GRE Board Research Rep. 85–17R). Princeton, NJ: Educational Testing Service.

Eysenck, H. J. (2003). Creativity, personality and the convergent-divergent continuum. In M. A. Runco (Ed.), *Perspectives on creativity research* (pp. 95–114). Cresskill: Hampton Press.

Fasko, D. (1999). Associative theory. In M. A. Runco & S. Pritzker (Eds.), *Encyclopedia of creativity* (Vol. I; pp. 135–139). San Diego: Academic Press.

Feist, G. J. (1998). A meta-analysis of personality in scientific and artistic creativity. *Personality and Social Psychology Review, 2,* 290–309.

Feist, G. J. & Barron, F. (2003). Predicting creativity from early to late adulthood: Intellect, potential, and personality. *Journal of Research in Personality, 37,* 62–88.

Feldhusen, J. F. (1998). A conception of talent and talent development. In R. C. Friedman & K. B. Rogers (Eds.), *Talent in context: Historical and social perspectives on giftedness* (pp. 193–209). Washington, DC: American Psychological Association.

Feldhusen, J. F., & Clinkenbeard, P. R. (1986). Creativity instructional materials: A review of research. *Journal of Creative Behavior, 20,* 153–182.

Finke, R. A. (1995). Creative insight and preinventive forms. In R. J. Sternberg & J. E. Davidson (Eds.), *The nature of insight* (pp. 255–280). Cambridge, MA: The MIT Press.

Finke, R. A., Ward, T. B., & Smith, S. M. (1992). *Creative cognition.* Cambridge, MA: MIT Press.

Fleenor, J. W. & Taylor, S. (1994). Construct validity of three self-report measures of creativity. *Educational and Psychological Measurement, 54,* 464–470.

Fuchs-Beauchamp, K. D., Karnes, M. B., & Johnson, L. J. (1993). Creativity and intelligence in preschoolers. *Gifted Child Quarterly, 37,* 113–117.

Furnham, A. (1999). Personality and creativity. *Perceptual and Motor Skills, 88,* 407–408.

Furnham, A. & Chamorro-Premuzic T. (2004). Estimating one's own personality and intelligence scores. *British Journal of Psychology, 95,* 145–160.

Furnham, A., Zhang, J., & Chamorro-Premuzic, T. (2006). The relationship between psychometric and self-estimated intelligence, creativity, personality, and academic achievement. *Cognition and Personality, 25,* 119–145.

Gallagher, A. M., & Kaufman, J. C. (Eds.). (2005). *Gender differences in mathematics.* Cambridge: Cambridge University Press.

Garcia, J. H. (2003). Nurturing creativity in Chicano populations: Integrating history, culture, family, and self. *Inquiry, 22,* 19–24.

Gardner, H. (1980) *Artful scribbles: The significance of children's drawings.* New York: Basic Books.

Gardner, H. (1983). *Frames of mind: the theory of multiple intelligences.* New York: Basic Books.

Gardner, H. (1988). Creativity: An interdisciplinary perspective. *Creativity Research Journal, 1,* 8–26.

Gardner, H. (1993a). *Creating minds: An anatomy of creativity seen through the lives of Freud, Einstein, Picasso, Stravinsky, Eliot, Graham, and Gandhi.* New York: Basic Books.

Gardner, H. (1995). Reflections on multiple intelligences: Myths and messages. *Phi Delta Kappan, 77,* 200–209.

Gardner, H. (1999). Intelligence reframed: Multiple intelligences for the 21st century. New York: Basic Books.

George, J. M. & Zhou, J. (2001). When openness to experience and conscientiousness are related to creative behavior: an interactional approach. *Journal of Applied Psychology, 86,* 513–524.

Getzels, J. W., & Jackson, P. W. (1962). *Creativity and intelligence: Explorations with gifted students.* New York: Wiley.

Gist, M. E., & Mitchell, T. R. (1992). Self-efficacy: A theoretical analysis of its determinants and malleability. *Academy of Management Review, 17,* 183–211.

Glover, J. A. (1976). Comparative levels of creative ability in Black and White college students. *Journal of Genetic Psychology, 128,* 95–99.

Goldberg, L. R. (1999). A broad-bandwidth, public domain, personality inventory measuring the lower-level facets of several five-factor models. In I. Mervielde, I. Deary, F. De Fruyt, & F. Ostendorf (Eds.), *Personality Psychology in Europe*, Vol. 7 (pp. 7–28). Tilburg, The Netherlands: Tilburg University Press.

Goldberg, L. R., Johnson, J. A., Eber, H. W., Hogan, R., Ashton, M. C., Cloninger, C. R., & Gough, H. C. (2006). The International Personality Item Pool and the future of public-domain personality measures. *Journal of Research in Personality, 40,* 84–96.

Goldberg, L. R., Sweeney, D., Meenda, P. F., & Hughes, J. E., Jr. (1998). Demographic variables and personality: The effects of gender, age, education, and ethnic/racial status on self-descriptions of personality attributes. *Personality and Individual Differences, 24,* 393–403.

Goldsmith, R. E. (1985). The factorial composition of the Kirton Adaption-Innovation Inventory. *Educational and Psychological Measurement, 45,* 245–250.

Goldsmith, R. E., & Matherly, T. A. (1988). Creativity and self-esteem: A multiple operationalization validity study. *Journal of Psychology, 122,* 47–56.

Gould, S. J. (1981). *The mismeasure of man.* New York: W. W. Norton.

Graef, R., Csikszentmihalyi, M., & Giannino, S. M. (1983). Measuring intrinsic motivation in everyday life. *Leisure Studies, 2,* 155–168.

Gridley, B. E., & Treloar, J. H. (1984). The validity of the Scales for Rating the Behavioral Characteristics of Superior Students for the identification of gifted students. *Journal of Psychoeducational Assessment, 2*(1), 65–71.

Griffin, M., & McDermott, M. R. (1998). Exploring a tripartite relationship between rebelliousness, openness to experience and creativity. *Social Behavior and Personality, 26,* 347–356.

Grohman, M., Wodniecka, Z., & Klusak, M. (2006). Divergent thinking and evaluation skills: Do they always go together? *Journal of Creative Behavior, 40,* 125–145.

Guilford, J. P. (1950). Creativity. *American Psychologist, 5,* 444–544.

Guilford, J. P. (1967). *The nature of human intelligence.* New York: McGraw-Hill.

Guilford, J. P. (1968). *Intelligence, creativity, and their educational implications.* San Diego: Robert R. Knapp.

Guilford, J. P. (1988). Some changes in the Structure-of-Intellect Model. *Educational and Psychological Measurement, 48,* 1–4.

Guilford, J. P., & Hoepfner, R. (1966). Sixteen divergent-production abilities at the ninth-grade level. *Multivariate Behavioral Research, 1,* 43–64.

Guillory, M., & Kher-Durlabhji, N. (1995, November). *Performance on the Torrance Test of Creative Thinking and Structure of Intellect-Learning Abilities Test: Is there a relationship?* Paper presented at the Annual Meeting of the Mid-South Educational Research Association, Biloxi, MS. (ERIC Document Reproduction Service No. ED 393 894)

Haensly, P. A., & Reynolds, C. R. (1989). Creativity and intelligence. In J. A. Glover, R. R. Ronning, & C. R. Reynolds (Eds.), *Handbook of creativity* (pp. 111–132). New York: Plenum Press.

Halpern, D. F. (2000). *Sex differences in cognitive abilities* (3rd ed.). Hillsdale, NJ: Erlbaum.

Hargreaves, D. J., Galton, M. J., & Robinson, S. (1996). Teachers' assessments of primary children's classroom work in the creative arts. *Educational Research, 38,* 199–211.

Harris, J. A. (2004). Measured intelligence, achievement, openness to experience, and creativity. *Personality and Individual Differences, 36,* 913–929.

Hattie, J. (1980). Should creativity tests be administered under testlike conditions? An empirical study of three alternative conditions. *Journal of Educational Psychology, 72,* 87–98.

Hattie, J., & Rogers, H. J. (1986). Factor models for assessing the relation between creativity and intelligence. *Journal of Educational Psychology, 78,* 482–485.

Hayes, J. R. (1989). Cognitive processes in creativity. In J. A. Glover, R. R. Ronning, & C. R. Reynolds (Eds.), *Handbook of creativity* (pp. 135–145). New York: Plenum Press.

Heausler, N. L., & Thompson, B. (1988). Structure of the Torrance Tests of Creative Thinking. *Educational and Psychological Measurement, 48,* 463–468.

Hébert, T. P., Cramond, B., Spiers-Neumeister, K. L., Millar, G., & Silvian, A. F. (2002). *E. Paul Torrance: His life, accomplishments, and legacy.* Storrs, CT: The University of Connecticut, National Research Center on the Gifted and Talented.

Helson, R. (1996). In search of the creative personality. *Creativity Research Journal, 9,* 295–306.

Helson, R., Roberts, B., & Agronick, G. (1995). Enduringness and change in creative personality and the prediction of occupational creativity. *Journal of Personality and Social Psychology, 69,* 1173–1183.

Henage, D., McCarney, S. B., & Anderson, P. D. (1998). *Gifted Evaluation Scale* (2nd ed.). Columbia, MO: Hawthorne Educational Services.

Hennessey, B. A. (1994). The consensual assessment technique: An examination of the relationship between ratings of product and process creativity. *Creativity Research Journal, 7,* 193–208.

Hennessey, B. A., & Amabile, T. M. (1999). Consensual assessment. In M. A. Runco & S. R. Pritzker (Eds.), *Encyclopedia of creativity, vol. 1* (pp. 346–359). San Diego: Academic Press.

Herrnstein, R. J., & Murray, C. (1994). *The bell curve.* New York: The Free Press.

Heuchert, J. W. P., Parker, W. D., Stumpf, H., & Myburgh, C. P. H. (2000). The Five-Factor Model in South African college students. *American Behavioral Scientist, 44,* 112–125.

Hickey, M. (2001). An application of Amabile's consensual assessment technique for rating the creativity of children's musical compositions. *Journal of Research in Music Education, 49,* 234–244.

Hocevar, D. (1979a). A comparison of statistical infrequency and subjective judgment as criteria in the measurement of originality. *Journal of Personality Assessment, 43,* 297–299.

Hocevar, D. (1979b, April). *The development of the Creative Behavior Inventory.* Paper presented at the annual meeting of the Rocky Mountain Psychological Association. (ERIC Document Reproduction Service No. ED 170 350)

Hocevar, D. (1979c). The unidimensional nature of creative thinking in fifth grade children. *Child Study Journal, 9,* 273–278.

Hocevar, D. (1979d). Ideational fluency as a confounding factor in the measurement of originality. *Journal of Educational Psychology, 71,* 191–196.

Hocevar, D. (1981). Measurement of creativity: Review and critique. *Journal of Personality Assessment, 45,* 450–464.

Hocevar, D., & Bachelor, P. (1989). A taxonomy and critique of measurements used in the study of creativity. In J. A. Glover, R. R. Ronning, & C. R. Reynolds (Eds.), *Handbook of creativity* (pp. 53–75). New York: Plenum Press.

Hocevar, D., & Michael, W. B. (1979). The effects of scoring formulas on the discriminant validity of tests of divergent thinking. *Educational and Psychological Measurement, 39,* 917–921.

Hofstee, W. K. B., de Raad, B., & Goldberg, L. R. (1992). Integration of the big five and circumplex approaches to trait structure. *Journal of Personality and Social Psychology, 63,* 146–163.

Holland, J. L. (1997). *Making vocational choices: A theory of vocational personalities and work environments* (3rd ed.). Odessa, FL: Psychological Assessment Resources.

Hollingworth, L. S. (1942). *Children above 180 IQ Stanford-Binet: Origin and development.* Yonkers, NY: World Book.

Holly, K. A., & Michael, W. B. (1972). The relationship of Structure-of-Intellect factor abilities to performance in high school modern algebra. *Educational and Psychological Measurement, 32,* 447–450.

Hong, E., Milgram, R. M., & Gorsky, H. (1995). Original thinking as a predictor of creative performance in young children. *Roeper Review, 18,* 147–149.

Horn, J. L., & Cattell, R. B. (*1966*). Refinement and test of the theory of fluid and crystallized intelligence. *Journal of Educational Psychology, 57,* 253–270.

Horn, J. L., & Noll, J. (1997). Human cognitive capacities: Gf-Gc theory. In D. P. Flanagan, J. L., Genshaft, & P. L. Harrison (Eds.), *Life-span developmental psychology: Research and theory* (pp. 423–466). New York: Academic Press.

Houtz, J. C., Shelby, E., Esquivel, G. B., Okoye, R. A., Peters, K. M., &

Treffinger, D. J. (2003). Creativity styles and personal type. *Creativity Research Journal,* 15, 321–330.

Howieson, N. (1981). A longitudinal study of creativity: 1965–1975. *Journal of Creative Behavior, 15,* 117–135.

Hu, W., & Adey, P. (2002). A scientific creativity test for secondary school students. *International Journal of Science Education, 24,* 389–404.

Hunsaker, S. L., & Callahan, C. M. (1995). Creativity and giftedness: Published instrument uses and abuses. *Gifted Child Quarterly, 39,* 110–114.

Ignatz, M. (1982). Sex differences in predictive ability of tests of Structure-of-Intellect factors relative to a criterion examination of high school physics achievement. *Educational and Psychological Measurement, 42,* 353–360.

International Personality Item Pool, *A Scientific Collaboratory for the Development of Advanced Measures of Personality Traits and Other Individual Differences.* Retrieved on from http://ipip.ori.org/

Isaken, S. G., & Dorval, K. B. (1993). Toward an improved understanding of creativity within people: The level-style distinction. In S. G. Isaksen, M. C. Murdock, R. L. Firestien, & D. J. Treffinger (Eds.), *Understanding and recognizing creativity: The emergence of a discipline* (pp. 299–330). Norwood, NJ: Ablex.

Iscoe, I., & Pierce-Jones, J. (1964). Divergent thinking, age, and intelligence in white and Negro children. *Child Development, 35,* 785–797.

Ivcevic, Z., & Mayer, J. D. (2007). Creative types and personality. *Imagination, Cognition, and Personality, 26,* 65–86.

Jacoby, R., & Glauberman, N. (1995). *The bell curve debate.* New York: Times Books.

Jaquish, G. A., & Ripple, R. E. (1984). A life-span developmental cross-cultural study of divergent thinking abilities. *International Journal of Aging & Human Development, 20,* 1–11.

Jaussi, K. S., Randel, A. E., & Dionne, S. D. (2007). I am, I think I can, and I do: The role of personal identity, self-efficacy, and cross-application of experiences in creativity at work. *Creativity Research Journal, 19,* 247–258.

Johnsen, S. K. (1997). Assessment beyond definitions. *Peabody Journal of Education, 72,* 136–152.

Johnsen, S. K. (2008). Identifying gifted and talented learners. In F. A. Karnes & K. R. Stephens (Eds.), *Achieving excellence: Educating the gifted and talented* (pp. 135–153). Upper Saddle River, NJ: Pearson Prentice Hall.

Johnson, L. D. (1985). Creative thinking potential: Another example of U-shaped development? *Creative Child and Adult Quarterly, 10,* 146–159.

Jones, W., Bellugi, U., Lai, Z., Chiles, M., Reilly, J., Lincoln, A., & Adolphs, R. (2000). Hypersociability in Williams syndrome. *Journal of Cognitive Neuroscience, 12,* 30–46.

Kaltsounis, B. (1974). Race, socioeconomic status and creativity. *Psychological Reports, 35,* 164–166.

Karnes, F. A., & Bean, S. M. (Ed.). (2001). *Methods and materials for teaching the gifted.* Waco, TX: Prufrock Press.

Kasof, J. (1997). Creativity and breadth of attention. *Creativity Research Journal, 10,* 303–315.

Kaufman, A. S., & Kaufman, N. L. (2004). *Kaufman Assessment Battery for Children—Second Edition (KABC-II) administration and scoring manual.* Circle Pines, MN: American Guidance Service.

Kaufman, J. C., & Baer, J. (2004). The Amusement Park Theoretical (APT) Model of creativity. *Korean Journal of Thinking and Problem Solving, 14,* 15–25.

Kaufman, J. C., & Baer, J. (Eds.). (2005). *Creativity across domains: Faces of the muse.* Mahwah, NJ: Lawrence Erlbaum.

Kaufman, J. C., & Baer, J. (2005). The amusement park theory of creativity. In J. C. Kaufman & J. Baer (Eds.), *Creativity across domains: Faces of the muse* (pp. 321–328). Hillsdale, NJ: Lawrence Erlbaum Associates.

Kaufman, J. C., & Baer, J. (Eds.). (2006). *Creativity and reason in cognitive development.* New York: Cambridge University Press.

Kaufman, J. C., & Baer, J. (2006). Intelligent testing with Torrance. *Creativity Research Journal, 18,* 99–102.

Kaufman, J. C., Baer, J., Cole, J. C., & Sexton, J. D. (in press). A comparison of expert and nonexpert raters using the Consensual Assessment Technique. *Creativity Research Journal.*

Kaufman, J. C., Baer, J., & Gentile, C. A. (2004). Differences in gender and ethnicity as measured by ratings of three writing tasks. *Journal of Creative Behavior, 39,* 56–69.

Kaufman, J. C., Cole, J. C., & Baer, J. (in press). The construct of creativity: Structural model for self-reported creativity ratings. *Journal of Creative Behavior.*

Kaufman, J. C., Gentile, C. A., & Baer, J. (2005). Do gifted student writers and creative writing experts rate creativity the same way? *Gifted Child Quarterly, 49,* 260–265.

Kaufman, J. C., & Kaufman, S. B. (2008). Creativity in intelligence tests. Manuscript in preparation.

Kaufman, J. C., Lee, J., Baer, J., & Lee, S. (2007). Captions, consistency, creativity, and the consensual assessment technique: New evidence of validity. *Thinking Skills and Creativity, 2*(2), 96–106.

Kaufman, J. C., Niu, W., Sexton, J. D., & Cole, J. C. (under review). In the eye of the beholder: Differences across ethnicity and gender in evaluating creative work.

Kaufman, J. C., & Sternberg, R. J. (Eds.). (2006). *The international handbook of creativity.* New York: Cambridge University Press.

Kessler, C., & Quinn, M. E. (1987). Language minority children's linguistic and cognitive creativity. *Journal of Multilingual and Multicultural Development, 8,* 173–186.

Kihlstrom, J. F., Shames, V. A., & Dorfman, J. (1996). Intimations of memory and thought. In L. Reder (Ed.), *Implicit memory and metacognition* (pp. 1–23). Mahwah, NJ: Erlbaum.

Kim, K. H. (2005). Can only intelligent people be creative? *Journal of Secondary Gifted Education, 16,* 57–66.

Kim, K. H. (2006). Is Creativity Unidimensional or multidimensional? Analyses of the Torrance Tests of Creative Thinking. *Creativity Research Journal, 18,* 251–259.

King, L. A., McKee-Walker, L., & Broyles, S. J. (1996). Creativity and the five factor model. *Journal of Research in Personality, 30,* 189–203.

Kirton, M. J. (Ed.). (1994a). *Adaptors and innovators: Styles of creativity and problem solving.* New York: Routledge.

Kirton, M. J. (1994b). A theory of cognitive style. In M. J. Kirton (Ed.),

Adaptors and innovators: Styles of creativity and problem solving (pp. 1–33). New York: Routledge.

Kirton, M. J. (1999). *Kirton Adaption-Innovation Inventory (KAI)*. (3rd ed.). Hertfordshire, UK: KAI Distribution Centre.

Kitano, M. K. (1999). Bringing clarity to "This thing called giftedness": A response to Dr. Renzulli. *Journal for the Education of the Gifted, 23,* 87–101.

Knox, B. J., & Glover, J. A. (1978). A note on preschool experience effects on achievement, readiness, and creativity. *Journal of Genetic Psychology, 132,* 151–152.

Kogan, N., & Pankove, E. (1974). Long-term predictive validity of divergent-thinking tests: Some negative evidence. *Journal of Educational Psychology, 66,* 802–810.

Kozbelt, A. (2005). Factors affecting aesthetic success and improvement in creativity: A case study of the musical genres of Mozart. *Psychology of Music, 33,* 235–255.

Kris, E. (1952). *Psychoanalytic exploration of art.* New York: International Universities Press.

Kruger, J. (1999). Lake Wobegone, be gone! The "below-average effect" and the egocentric nature of comparative ability judgments. *Journal of Personality and Social Psychology, 77,* 221–232.

Kruger, J., & Dunning, D. (1999). Unskilled and unaware of it: How difficulties in recognizing one's own incompetence lead to inflated self-assessments. *Journal of Personality and Social Psychology, 77,* 1121–1134.

Kumar, V. K., & Holman, E. (1989). *Creativity Styles Questionnaire.* Unpublished instrument.

Kumar, V. K., Holman, E. R., & Rudegeair, P. (1991). Creativity styles of freshmen students. *Journal of Creative Behavior, 25,* 320–323.

Kumar, V. K., Kemmler, D., & Holman, E. R. (1997). The Creativity Styles Questionnaire-Revised. *Creativity Research Journal, 10,* 51–58.

Kyllonen, P. C., Walters, A. M., & Kaufman, J. C. (2005). Noncognitive constructs and their assessment in graduate education. *Educational Assessment, 10*(3), 153–184.

LaFrance, E. B. (1997). The gifted/dyslexic child: Characterizing and addressing strengths and weaknesses. *Annals of Dyslexia, 47,* 163–182.

Larson, R., & Csikszentmihalyi, M. (1983). The experience sampling method. In H. T. Reiss (Ed.), *Naturalistic approaches to studying social interaction. New directions for methodology of social and behavioral sciences* (pp. 41–56). San Francisco: Jossey-Bass.

Lee, J., Day, J. D., Meara, N. M., & Maxwell, S. E. (2002). Discrimination of social knowledge and its flexible application from creativity: A multitrait-multimethod approach. *Personality and Individual Differences, 32,* 913–928.

Leroux, J. A., & Levitt-Perlman, M. (2000). The gifted child with Attention Deficit Disorder: An identification and intervention challenge. *Roeper Review, 22,* 171–176.

Levinson, E. M., & Folino, L. (1994). Correlations of scores on the Gifted Evaluation Scale with those on WISC-III and Kaufman Brief Intelligence Test for students referred for gifted evaluation. *Psychological Reports, 74* (2), 419–424.

Licuanan, B. F., Dailey, L. R., & Mumford, M. D. (2007). Idea evaluation: Error in evaluating highly original ideas. *Journal of Creative Behavior, 41,* 1–27.

Lim, W., & Plucker, J. (2001). Creativity through a lens of social responsibility: Implicit theories of creativity with Korean samples. *Journal of Creative Behavior, 35,* 115–130.

Lin, C., Hu, W., Adey, P., & Shen, J. (2003). The influence of CASE on scientific creativity. *Research in Science Education, 33,* 143–162.

Lonergan, D. C., Scott, G. M., & Mumford, M. D. (2004). Evaluative aspects of creative thought: Effects of appraisal and revision standards. *Creativity Research Journal, 16,* 231–246.

Losh, M., Bellugi, U., Reilly, J., & Anderson, D. (2000). Narrative as a social engagement tool: The excessive use of evaluation in narratives from children with Williams syndrome. *Narrative Inquiry, 10,* 265–290.

Ludwig, A. M. (1995). The *price of greatness.* New York: Guilford.

Luria, A. R. (1966). *Human brain and psychological processes.* New York: Harper & Row.

Luria, A. R. (1970). The functional organization of the brain. *Scientific American, 222,* 66–78.

Luria, A. R. (1973). *The working brain: An introduction to neuropsychology.* London: Penguin.

MacKinnon, D. W. (1962). The nature and nurture of creative talent. *American Psychologist, 17,* 484–495.

MacKinnon, D. W. (1965). Personality and the realization of creative potential. *American Psychologist, 20,* 273–281.

MacKinnon, D. W. (1978). In search of human effectiveness: Identifying and developing creativity. Buffalo, NY: Bearly Limited.

Marland, S. (1972). *Education of the gifted and talented* (Report to the Congress of the United States by the U. S. Commissioner of Education). Washington, DC: U.S. Government Printing Office.

Martinsen, Ø. (1995). Cognitive styles and experience in solving insight problems: Replication and extension. *Creativity Research Journal, 6,* 435–447.

Masten, W. G., Plata, M., Wenglar, K., & Thedford, J. (1999). Acculturation and Teacher Ratings of Hispanic and Anglo-American Students. *Roeper Review, 22,* 64–65.

Matud, M. P., Rodríguez, C., & Grande, J. (2007). Gender differences in creative thinking. *Personality and Individual Differences, 43,* 1137–1147.

Mayer, J. D. (2001). *On new methods of personality assessment.* Paper presented at the Symposium on Noncognitive Assessments for Graduate Admissions. Toronto, Canada: Graduate Record Examination Board.

Mayer, M., & Mayer, M. (1971). *A boy, a dog, a frog, and a friend.* New York: Dial Books.

McCrae, R. R. (1987). Creativity, divergent thinking, and openness to experience. *Journal of Personality and Social Psychology, 52,* 1258–1265.

McCrae, R. R., & Costa, P. T., Jr. (1997). Personality trait structure as a human universal. *American Psychologist, 52,* 509–516.

McGrew, K. S. (2005). The Cattell-Horn-Carroll Theory of Cognitive Abilities: Past, present, and future. In D. P. Flanagan & P. L. Harrison (Eds.), *Contemporary Intellectual Assessment* (pp. 136–182). New York: Guilford.

Mednick, S. A. (1962). The associative basis of the creative process. *Psychological Review, 69,* 220–232.

Mednick, S. A. (1968). The Remote Associates Test. *Journal of Creative Behavior, 2,* 213–214.

Meeker, M. (1987). *Meeker Creativity Rating Scale.* Vida, OR: SOI Systems.

Meeker, M., & Meeker, R. (1982). *Structure-of-Intellect Learning Abilities Test: Evaluation, leadership, and creative thinking.* El Segundo, CA: SOI Institute.

Meeker, M., Meeker, R., & Roid, G. H. (1985). *Structure-of-Intellect Learning Abilities Test (SOI-LA) manual.* Los Angeles: Western Psychological Services.

Meeker, M. N. (1969). *The structure of intellect: Its interpretation and uses.* Columbus, OH: Merrill.

Michael, W. B., & Bachelor, P. (1992). First-order and higher-order creative ability factors in Structure-of-Intellect measures administered to sixth-grade children. *Educational and Psychological Measurement, 52,* 261–273.

Milgram, R. M., & Hong, E. (1993). Creative thinking and creative performance in adolescents as predictors of creative attainments in adults: A follow-up study after 18 years. *Roeper Review, 15,* 135–139.

Milgram, R. M., & Hong, E. (1994). Creative thinking and creative performance in adolescents as predictors of creative attainments in adults: A follow-up study after 18 years. In R. F. Subotnik & K. D. Arnold (Eds.), *Beyond Terman: Contemporary longitudinal studies of giftedness and talent* (p. 212–228). Norwood, NJ: Ablex.

Milgram, R. M., & Milgram, N. A. (1976). Creative thinking and creative performance in Israeli students. *Journal of Educational Psychology, 68,* 255–259.

Milgram, R. M., & Rabkin, L. (1980). Developmental test of Mednick's associative hierarchies of original thinking. *Developmental Psychology, 16,* 157–158.

Mönks, F. J., & Mason, E. J. (1993). Developmental theories and giftedness. In K. A. Heller, F. J. Mönks, & A. H. Passow (Eds.), *International handbook of research and development of giftedness and talent* (pp. 89–101). New York: Pergamon Press.

Myford, C. M. (1989). *The nature of expertise in aesthetic judgment: beyond inter-judge agreement.* Unpublished doctoral dissertation, University of Georgia.

Naglieri, J. A. (2005). The Cognitive Assessment System. In D. P. Flanagan & P. L. Harrison (Eds.), *Contemporary intellectual assessment* (pp. 441–460). New York: Guilford.

Naglieri, J. A., & Das, J. P. (2005). Planning, Attention, Simultaneous, Successive (PASS) Theory: A revision of the concept of intelligence. In D. P. Flanagan & P. L. Harrison (Eds.), *Contemporary intellectual assessment* (pp. 120–135). New York: Guilford.

Naglieri, J. A., & Kaufman, J. C. (2001). Understanding intelligence, giftedness, and creativity using PASS theory. *Roeper Review, 23,* 151–156.

Nickerson, R. S. (1999). Enhancing creativity. In R. J. Sternberg (Ed.), *Handbook of creativity.* (pp. 392–430). Cambridge, UK: Cambridge University Press.

Niu, W. (2007). Individual and environmental influences on Chinese student creativity. *Journal of Creative Behavior, 41,* 151–175.

Niu, W. & Sternberg, R. J. (2001) Cultural influence of artistic creativity and its evaluation. *International Journal of Psychology, 36*(4), 225–241.

Nettle, D. (2006). Psychological profiles of professional actors. *Personality and Individual Differences, 40,* 375–383.

Office of Educational Research and Improvement (1993). *National excellence: A case study for developing America's talent.* Washington, DC: U.S. Government Printing Office.

Okuda, S. M., Runco, M. A., & Berger, D. E. (1991). Creativity and the finding and solving of real-world problems. *Journal of Psychoeducational Assessment, 9,* 45–53.

Olszewski-Kubilius, P. (1999). A critique of Renzulli's theory into practice models for gifted learners. *Journal for the Education of the Gifted, 23,* 55–66.

O'Quin, K., & Besemer, S. P. (1989). The development, reliability, and validity of the revised creative product semantic scale. Creativity Research Journal, *2,* 267–278.

Oral, G., Kaufman, J. C., & Agars, M. D. (2007). Examining creativity in Turkey: Do Western findings apply? *High Ability Studies 18,* 235–246.

Osborn, A. A. (1963). Applied *imagination* (3rd ed.). New York: Charles Scribner's.

Paguio, L. P. (1983). The influence of gender of child and parent on perceptions of the ideal child. *Child Study Journal, 13,* 187–194.

Palaniappan, A. K. (1996). A cross-cultural study of creative perceptions. *Perceptual and Motor Skills, 82,* 96–98.

Palaniappan, A. K., & Torrance, E. P. (2001). Comparison between regular and streamlined versions of scoring of Torrance Tests of Creative Thinking. *Korean Journal of Thinking & Problem Solving, 11,* 5–7.

Park, M., Lee, J., & Hahn, D. W. (2002). *Self-reported creativity, creativity, and intelligence.* Poster presented at the American Psychological Association, Chicago.

Parnes, S. J., Noller, R. B., & Biondi, A. M. (1977). *Guide to creative action.* New York: Scribner's.

Passow, A. H. (1979). A look around and a look ahead. In A. H. Passow (Ed.), *The gifted and talented: Their education and development, the 78th yearbook of the National Society for the Study of Education* (pp. 447–451). Chicago, IL: NSSE.

Passow, A. H., & Rudnitski, R. A. (1993). *State policies regarding education of the gifted as reflected in legislation and regulation* (CRS93302). Storrs, CT: The National Research Center on the Gifted and Talented, University of Connecticut.

Paulhus, D. L., Lysy, D., & Yik, M. (1998). Self-report measures of intelligence: Are they useful as proxy measures of IQ? *Journal of Personality, 64,* 525–555.

Paulos, J. A. (1988). *Innumeracy: Mathematical illiteracy and its consequences.* New York: Vintage Books.

Pearlman, C. (1983). Teachers as an informational resource in identifying and rating student creativity. *Education, 103*(3), 215–222.

Perrine, N. E., & Brodersen, R. M. (2005). Artistic and scientific creative behavior: Openness and the mediating role of interests. *Journal of Creative Behavior, 39,* 217–236.

Perry, S. K. (1999). *Writing in flow.* Cincinnati, OH: Writer's Digest Books.

Phillips, V. K. (1973). Creativity: Performance, profiles, and perceptions. *Journal of Psychology: Interdisciplinary and Applied, 83,* 25–30.

Piirto, J. A. (2004). *Understanding creativity.* Scottsdale, AZ: Great Potential Press.

Pinker, S., & Spelke, E. (April 22, 2005). *The science of gender and science: Pinker vs. Spelke: A debate sponsored by Harvard's Mind Brain and Behavior Inter-Faculty Initiative.* Retrieved May 11, 2006, from the Edge Foundation Website: http://www.edge.org/3rd_culture/debate05/debate05_index.html

Plucker, J. A. (1998). Beware of simple conclusions: The case for the content generality of creativity. *Creativity Research Journal, 11,* 179–182.

Plucker, J. (1999a). Is the proof in the pudding? Reanalyses of Torrance's (1958 to present) longitudinal study data. *Creativity Research Journal, 12,* 103–114.

Plucker, J. (1999b). Reanalyses of student responses to creativity checklists: Evidence of content generality. *Journal of Creative Behavior, 33,* 126–137.

Plucker, J. (2000). Flip sides of the same coin or marching to the beat of different drummers? A response to Pyryt. *Gifted Child Quarterly, 44,* 193–195.

Plucker, J. (2005). The (relatively) generalist view of creativity. In J. C. Kaufman & J. Baer (Eds.), *Creativity across domains: Faces of the muse* (pp. 307–312). Mahwah, NJ: Lawrence Erlbaum Associates.

Plucker, J. A. & Beghetto, R. A. (2004). Why creativity is domain general, why it looks domain specific, and why the distinction does not matter. In R. J. Sternberg, E. L. Grigorenko, & J. L. Singer (Eds.), *Creativity: From potential to realization.* Washington DC: American Psychological Association.

Plucker, J., Beghetto, R. A., & Dow, G. (2004). Why isn't creativity more important to educational psychologists? Potential, pitfalls, and future directions in creativity research. *Educational Psychologist, 39,* 83–96.

Plucker, J., Callahan, C. M., & Tomchin, E. M. (1996). Wherefore art thou, multiple intelligences? Alternative assessments for identifying talent in ethnically diverse and economically disadvantaged students. *Gifted Child Quarterly, 40,* 81–92.

Plucker, J., & Renzulli, J. S. (1999). Psychometric approaches to the study of human creativity. In R. J. Sternberg (Ed.), *Handbook of creativity* (pp. 35–60). New York: Cambridge University Press.

Plucker, J., & Runco, M. (1998). The death of creativity measurement has been greatly exaggerated: Current issues, recent advances, and future directions in creativity assessment. *Roeper Review, 21,* 36–39.

Plucker, J., Runco, M., & Lim, W. (2006). Predicting ideational behavior from divergent thinking and discretionary time on task. *Creativity Research Journal, 18,* 55–63.

Pornrungroj, C. (1992). A comparison of creativity test scores between Thai children in a Thai culture and Thai-American children who were born and reared in an American culture. Unpublished doctoral dissertation, Illinois State University.

Preckel, F., Holling, H., & Wiese, M. (2006). Relationship of intelligence and creativity in gifted and non-gifted students: An investigation of threshold theory. *Personality and Individual Differences, 40,* 159–170.

Prescott, S., Csikszentmihalyi, M., & Graef, R. (1981). Environmental effects on cognitive and affective states: The experiential time sampling approach. *Social Behavior and Personality, 9,* 23–32.

Powers, D. E., & Kaufman, J. C. (2004). Do standardized tests penalize deep-thinking, creative, or conscientious students? Some personality correlates of Graduate Record Examinations test scores. *Intelligence, 32,* 145–153.

Pretz, J. E., & Totz, K. S. (2007). Measuring individual differences in affective, heuristic, and holistic intuition. *Personality and Individual Differences, 43,* 1247–1257.

Price-Williams, D. R., & Ramirez III, M. (1977). Divergent thinking, cultural differences, and bilingualism. *The Journal of Social Psychology, 103,* 3–11.

Priest, T. (2006). Self-evaluation, creativity, and musical achievement. *Psychology of Music, 34,* 47–61.

Proctor, R. M. J., & Burnett, P. C. (2004). Measuring cognitive and dispositional characteristics of creativity in elementary students. *Creativity Research Journal, 16,* 421–429.

Pyryt, M. C. (2000). Finding "g": Easy Viewing through Higher Order Factor Analysis. *Gifted Child Quarterly, 44,* 190–92.

Rack, L. (1981). Developmental dyslexia and literary creativity: Creativity in the area of deficit. *Journal of Learning Disabilities, 14,* 262–263.

Ramos-Ford, V., & Gardner, H. (1997). Giftedness from a multiple intelligences perspective. In N. Colangelo & G. A. David (Eds.), *Handbook of gifted education,* (2nd ed.). Boston: Allyn & Bacon.

Randel, A. E. and Jaussi, K. S. (2003). Functional background identity, diversity, and individual performance in cross-functional teams. *Academy of Management Journal, 46,* 763–774.

Rawashdeh, I., & Al-Qudah, B. (2003). Effect of cooperative instruction method on promoting creative thinking of the eighth elementary students. *Dirasat: Educational Sciences, 30*(2).

Reffel, J. A. (2003). Creative teachers value creative characteristics in their students. *Center for Creative Learning Newsletter, 12*(1), 2–4.

Reich, R. B. (July 20, 2001). Standards for what? *Education Week, 20,* 64.

Reilly, J., Klima, E. S., & Bellugi, U. (1990). Once more with feeling: Affect and language in atypical populations. *Development and Psychopathology, 2,* 367–391.

Reis, S. M., & Renzulli, J. S. (1991). The assessment of creative products in programs for gifted and talented students. *Gifted Child Quarterly, 35,* 128–134.

Renzulli, J. S. (1973). *New directions in creativity.* New York: Harper & Row.

Renzulli, J. S. (1978). What makes giftedness? Reexamining a definition. *Phi Delta Kappan, 60,* 180–184, 261.

Renzulli, J. S. (Ed.). (1984). *Technical report of research studies related to the Revolving Door Identification Model* (2nd ed.). Storrs, CT: Bureau of Educational Research and Service, The University of Connecticut.

Renzulli, J. S. (1986). The three-ring conception of giftedness: A developmental model for creative productivity. In Sternberg, R. J., & Davidson, J. (Eds.), *Conceptions of giftedness* (pp. 53–92). New York: Cambridge University Press.

Renzulli, J. S. (Ed.). (1988). *Technical report of research studies related to the Revolving Door Identification Model* (2nd ed., Vol. II). Storrs, CT: Bureau of Educational Research and Service, The University of Connecticut.

Renzulli, J. S. (1999). Reflections, perceptions, and future directions. *Journal for the Education of the Gifted, 23,* 125–146.

Renzulli, J. S. (2005). The three-ring definition of giftedness: A developmental model for promoting creative productivity. In R. J. Sternberg & J. E. Davidson (Eds.), *Conceptions of giftedness* (2nd ed., pp. 246–280). New York: Cambridge University Press.

Renzulli, J. S., Owen, S. V., & Callahan, C. M. (1974). Fluency, flexibility, and originality as a function of group size. *Journal of Creative Behavior, 8,* 107–113.

Renzulli, J. S., & Reis, S. M. (1985). *The schoolwide enrichment model: A comprehensive plan for educational excellence.* Mansfield Center, CT: Creative Learning Press.

Renzulli, J. S., Smith, L. H., White, A. J., Callahan, C. M., Hartman, R. K., Westberg, K. L., Gavin, M. K., Reis, S. M., Siegle, D., & Sytsma, R. E. (2004). *Scales for Rating the Behavioral Characteristics of Superior Students.* Mansfield Center, CT: Creative Learning Press.

Rhodes, M. (1961). An analysis of creativity. *Phi Delta Kappan, 42,* 305–311.

Richardson, A. G. (1985). Sex differences in creativity among a sample of Jamaican adolescents. *Perceptual and Motor Skills, 60,* 424–426.

Rimm, S. B. (1983). *Preschool and Kindergarten Interest Descriptor.* Watertown, WI: Educational Assessment Systems.

Robinson, N. M., Zigler, E., & Gallagher, J. J. (2000). Two tails of the normal curve: Similarities and differences in the study of mental retardation and giftedness. *American Psychologist, 55,* 1413–1424.

Robinson, N. M. (2005). In defense of a psychometric approach to the definition of academic giftedness: A conservative view from a die-hard liberal. In R. J. Sternberg & J. E. Davidson (Eds.), *Conceptions of giftedness* (2nd ed., pp. 280–294). New York: Cambridge University Press.

Roid, G. H. (2003). *Stanford-Binet Intelligence Scales* (5th ed.). Itasca, IL: Riverside.

Rose, L. H., & Lin, H. (1984). A meta-analysis of long-term creativity training programs. *Journal of Creative Behavior, 18,* 11–22.

Rosen, C. L. (1985). Test review of Creativity Assessment Packet. From J. V. Mitchell, Jr. (Ed.), *The ninth mental measurements yearbook* [Electronic version]. Retrieved January 9, 2008, from the Buros Institute's *Test Reviews Online* website: http://www.unl.edu/buros

Ross, S. R. (1999). Clarifying the construct of schizotypy: Variability as a marker of subtype. *Dissertation Abstracts International, 60*(06), 3003B.

Rostan, S. M., Pariser, D., & Gruber, H. E. (2002). A cross-cultural study of the development of artistic talent, creativity, and giftedness. *High Ability Studies, 13,* 125–156.

Rotter, D. M., Langland, L., & Berger, D. (1971). The validity of tests of creative thinking in seven-year-old children. *Gifted Child Quarterly, 4,* 273–278.

Rudowicz, E., Lok, D., & Kitto, J. (1995). Use of the Torrance Tests of Creative Thinking in an exploratory study of creativity in Hong Kong primary school children: A cross-cultural comparison. *International Journal of Psychology, 30,* 417–430.

Runco, M. A. (1984). Teachers' judgments of creativity and social validation of divergent thinking tests. *Perceptual and Motor Skills, 59,* 711–717.

Runco, M. A. (1985). Reliability and convergent validity of ideational flexibility as a function of academic achievement. *Perceptual and Motor Skills, 61,* 1075–1081.

Runco, M. A. (1986a). The discriminant validity of gifted children's divergent thinking test scores. *Gifted Child Quarterly, 30,* 78–82.

Runco, M. A. (1986b). Divergent thinking and creative performance in gifted and nongifted children. *Educational and Psychological Measurement, 46,* 375–384.

Runco, M. A. (1986c). Maximal performance on divergent thinking tests by gifted, talented, and nongifted children. *Psychology in the Schools, 23,* 308–315.

Runco, M. A. (1987). The generality of creative performance in gifted and nongifted children. *Gifted Child Quarterly, 31,* 121–125.

Runco, M. A. (1989a). Parents' and teachers' ratings of the creativity of children. *Journal of Social Behavior and Personality, 4,* 73–83.

Runco, M. A. (1989b). The creativity of children's art. *Child Study Journal, 19,* 177–190.

Runco, M. A. (Ed.). (1991). *Divergent thinking.* Norwood, NJ: Ablex.

Runco, M. A. (1992a). Children's divergent thinking and creative ideation. *Developmental Review, 12,* 233–264.

Runco, M. A. (1992b). The evaluative, valuative, and divergent thinking of children. *Journal of Creative Behavior, 25,* 311–319.

Runco, M. A. (1993a). *Creativity as an educational objective for disadvantaged students* (Report Number 9306). Storrs, CT: National Research Center on the Gifted and Talented.

Runco, M. A. (1993b). Divergent thinking, creativity, and giftedness. *Gifted Child Quarterly, 37,* 16–22.

Runco, M. A. (1999) Divergent thinking. In M. A. Runco & S. Pritzker (Eds.), *Encyclopedia of creativity* (Vol. I; pp. 577–582). San Diego: Academic Press.

Runco, M. A. (2002). Parents' and teachers' implicit theories of children's creativity: A cross-cultural perspective. *Creativity Research Journal, 14,* 427–438.

Runco, M. A. (2005). Creative giftedness. In R. J. Sternberg & J. E. Davidson (Eds.), *Conceptions of giftedness* (2nd ed., pp. 295–311). New York: Cambridge University Press.

Runco, M. A. (2007). *Creativity: Theories and themes: Research, development, and practice.* New York: Academic Press.

Runco, M. A. (in press). Divergent thinking is not synonymous with creativity: Comments on "Assessing creativity with divergent thinking tasks: Exploring the reliability and validity of new subjective scoring methods." *Psychology of Aesthetics, Creativity, and the Arts.*

Runco, M. A. (in press). *Divergent thinking and creative ideation.* Cresskill, NJ: Hampton Press.

Runco, M. A., & Albert, R. S. (1985). The reliability and validity of ideational originality in the divergent thinking of academically gifted and nongifted children. *Educational and Psychological Measurement, 45,* 483–501.

Runco, M. A., & Chand, I. (1994). Problem finding, evaluative thinking, and creativity. In M. A. Runco (Ed.), *Problem finding, problem solving, and creativity* (pp. 40–76). Norwood, NJ: Ablex Publishing.

Runco, M. A., & Charles, R. E. (1993). Judgments of originality and appropriateness as predictors of creativity. *Personality and Individual Differences, 15,* 537–546.

Runco, M. A., & Dow, G. T. (2004). Assessing the accuracy of judgments of originality on three divergent thinking tests. *Korean Journal of Thinking & Problem Solving, 14,* 5–14.

Runco, M. A., Illies, J. J., & Reiter-Palmon, R. (2005). Explicit instructions to be creative and original: A comparison of strategies and criteria as targets with three types of divergent thinking tests. *Korean Journal of Thinking & Problem Solving, 15,* 5–15.

Runco, M. A., Johnson, D. J., & Bear, P. K. (1993). Parents' and teachers' implicit theories of children's creativity. *Child Study Journal, 23,* 91–113.

Runco, M. A., McCarthy, K. A., & Svenson, E. (1994). Judgments of the creativity of artwork from students and professional artists. *The Journal of Psychology, 128,* 23–31.

Runco, M. A., & Mraz, W. (1992). Scoring divergent thinking tests using total ideational output and a creativity index. *Educational and Psychological Measurement, 52,* 213–221.

Runco, M. A., Okuda, S. M., & Thurston, B. J. (1987). The psychometric properties of four systems for scoring divergent thinking tests. *Journal of Psychoeducational Assessment, 5,* 149–156.

Runco, M. A., & Okuda, S. M. (1988). Problem finding, divergent thinking, and the creative process. *Journal of Youth and Adolescence, 17,* 211–220.

Runco, M. A., & Okuda, S. M. (1991). The instructional enhancement of the flexibility and originality scores of divergent thinking tests. *Applied Cognitive Psychology, 5,* 435–441.

Runco, M. A. , Plucker, J., & Lim, W. (2000–2001). Development and psychometric integrity of a measure of ideational behavior. *Creativity Research Journal, 13,* 393–400.

Runco, M. A., & Smith, W. R. (1992). Interpersonal and intrapersonal evaluations of creative ideas. *Personality and Individual Differences, 13,* 295–302.

Runco, M. A., & Vega, L. (1990). Evaluating the creativity of children's ideas. *Journal of Social Behavior & Personality, 5,* 439–452.

Ruscio, J., Whitney, D. M., & Amabile, T. M. (1998). Looking inside the fishbowl of creativity: Verbal and behavioral predictors of creative performance. *Creativity Research Journal, 11,* 243–263.

Rust, J. O. (1985). Test review of Scales For Rating the Behavioral Characteristics of Superior Students. From J. V. Mitchell, Jr. (Ed.), *The ninth mental measurements yearbook* [Electronic version]. Retrieved January 9, 2008, from the Buros Institute's *Test Reviews Online* website: http://www.unl.edu/buros

Ryser, G. R. (2007). *Profiles of Creative Abilities: Examiner's manual.* Austin, TX: Pro-Ed.

Saeki, N., Fan, X., & Van Dusen, L. (2001.) A comparative study of creative thinking of American and Japanese college students. *Journal of Creative Behavior, 35,* 24–36.

Saucier, G., & Goldberg, L. R. (2001). Lexical studies of indigenous personality: Premises, products, and prospects. *Journal of Personality, 69,* 847–879.

Sawyer, R. K. (2006). *Explaining creativity: The science of human innovation.* Oxford: Oxford University Press.

Sawyers, J. K., & Canestaro, N. C. (1989). Creativity and achievement in design coursework. *Creativity Research Journal, 2,* 126–133.

Schmitt, D. P., Allik, J., McCrae, R. R., & Benet-Martínez, V. (in press). The geographic distribution of Big Five personality traits: Patterns and profiles of human self-description across 56 nations. *Journal of Cross-Cultural Psychology.*

Seddon, G. M. (1983). The measurement and properties of divergent thinking ability as a single compound entity. *Journal of Educational Measurement, 20,* 393–402.

Selby, E. C., Treffinger, D. J., Isaksen, S. G., & Powers, S. V. (1993). Use of the Kirton Adaption-Innovation Inventory with middle school students. *Journal of Creative Behavior, 27,* 223–235.

Shaw, G. A. (1992). Hyperactivity and creativity: The tacit dimension. *Bulletin of the Psychonomic Society, 30,* 157–160.

Shaw, G. A., & Brown, G. (1990). Laterality and creativity concomitants of attention problems. *Developmental Neuropsychology, 6,* 39–56.

Shaw, G. A., & Brown, G. (1991). Laterality, implicit memory and attention disorder. *Educational Studies, 17,* 15–23.

Silvia, P. J., Winterstein, B. P., Willse, J. T., Barona, C. M. , Cram, J. T., Hess, K. I., Martinez, J. L., & Richard, C. A. (in press). Assessing creativity with divergent thinking tasks: Exploring the reliability and validity of new subjective scoring methods. *Psychology of Aesthetics, Creativity, and the Arts.*

Simonton, D. K. (1994). *Greatness: Who makes history and why.* New York: Guilford.

Simonton, D. K. (2004). *Creativity in Science: Chance, Logic, Genius, and Zeitgeist.* Cambridge: Cambridge University Press.

Sligh, A. C., Conners, F. A., & Roskos-Ewoldsen, B. (2005). Relation of creativity to fluid and crystallized intelligence. *Journal of Creative Behavior, 39,* 123–136.

Smith, D. K. (1998). Test review of Gifted Education Scale (2nd ed.). In B. S. Plake & J. C. Impara (Eds.), *The fourteenth mental measurements yearbook* [Electronic version]. Retrieved January 9, 2008, from the Buros Institute's *Test Reviews Online* website: http://www.unl.edu/buros

Smith, S. M., & Blankenship, S. E. (1991). Incubation and the persistence of fixation in problem solving. *American Journal of Psychology, 104,* 61–87.

Snyder, A., Mitchell, J., Bossomaier, T., & Pallier, G. (2004). The creativity quotient: An objective scoring of ideational fluency. *Creativity Research Journal, 16,* 415–420.

Soldz, S. & Vaillant, G. E. (1999). The Big Five personality traits and the life course: A 50-year longitudinal study. *Journal of Research in Personality, 33,* 208–232.

Spearman, C. (1904). General intelligence, objectively determined and measured. *American Journal of Psychology, 15,* 201–293.

Standards for the English / Language Arts: A Project of the International Reading Association and the National Council of Teachers of English (1996). Newark, DE & Urbana, IL: IRA & NCTE.

Stanley, J. C. (1980). On educating the gifted. *Educational Researcher, 9,* 8–12.

Stanley, J. C., & Benbow, C. P. (1981). Using the SAT to find intellectually talented seventh graders. *College Board Review, 122,* 2–7, 26–27.

Stemler, S. E., Grigorenko, E. L., Jarvin, L., & Sternberg, R. J. (2006). Using the theory of successful intelligence as a basis for augmenting AP exams in psychology and statistics. *Contemporary Educational Psychology, 31,* 344–376.

Sternberg, R. J. (1993). *Sternberg Triarchic Abilities Test.* Unpublished test.

Sternberg, R. J. (1996). *Successful intelligence.* New York: Simon & Schuster.

Sternberg, R. J. (Ed.) (1999a). *Handbook of Creativity.* Cambridge: Cambridge University Press.

Sternberg, R. J. (Ed.). (1999b). *The nature of cognition.* Cambridge, MA: The MIT Press.

Sternberg, R. J. (1999c). The theory of successful intelligence. *Review of General Psychology, 3,* 292–316.

Sternberg, R. J. (2003). *WICS: Wisdom, Intelligence, and Creativity, Synthesized.* Cambridge: Cambridge University Press.

Sternberg, R. J. & Clinkenbeard, P. R. (1995). A triarchic model applied to identifying, teaching, and assessing gifted children. *Roeper Review, 17,* 255–260.

Sternberg, R. J., & Davidson, J. E. (Eds.). (1986). *Conceptions of giftedness.* New York: Cambridge University Press.

Sternberg, R. J., Ferrari, M., Clinkenbeard, P. R., & Grigorenko, E. L. (1996). Identification, instruction, and assessment of gifted children: A construct validation of a triarchic model, *Gifted Child Quarterly, 40,* 129–137.

Sternberg, R. J., & Grigorenko, E. L. (2000–2001). Guilford's Structure of Intellect model and model of creativity: Contributions and limitations. *Creativity Research Journal, 13,* 309–316.

Sternberg, R. J., Grigorenko, E. L., Ferrari, M., & Clinkenbeard, P. (1999). A triarchic analysis of an aptitude-treatment interaction. *European Journal of Psychological Assessment, 15,* 1–11.

Sternberg, R. J., Grigorenko, E. L., Singer, J. L. (Eds.) (2004). *Creativity: From potential to realization.* Washington, DC: American Psychological Association.

Sternberg, R. J., Kaufman, J. C., & Grigorenko, E. L. (2008). *Applied intelligence.* Cambridge: Cambridge University Press.

Sternberg, R. J., Kaufman, J. C., & Pretz, J. E. (2002). *The creativity conundrum.* Philadelphia: Psychology Press.

Sternberg, R. J., & Lubart, T. I. (1995). *Defying the crowd.* New York: Free Press.

Sternberg, R. J., & O'Hara, L. A. (1999). Creativity and intelligence. In R. J. Sternberg (Ed.), *Handbook of creativity* (pp. 251–272). New York: Cambridge University Press.

Sternberg, R. J., & the Rainbow Project Collaborators (2006). The Rainbow Project: Enhancing the SAT through assessments of analytical, practical and creative skills. *Intelligence, 34,* 321–350.

Sternberg, R. J., Torff, B., & Grigorenko, E. L. (1998a). Teaching for successful intelligence raises school achievement. *Phi Delta Kappan, 79,* 667–669.

Sternberg, R. J., Torff, B., & Grigorenko, E. L. (1998b). Teaching triarchically improves school achievement. *Journal of Educational Psychology, 90,* 374–384.

Stokes, P. D. (2005). *Creativity from constraints: The psychology of breakthrough.* New York, NY: Springer Publishing.

Strough, J., & Diriwaechter, R. (2000). Dyad gender differences in preadolescents' creative stories. *Sex Roles, 43,* 43–60.

Sulloway, F. J. (1996). *Born to rebel.* New York: Vintage.

Swartz, J. D. (1988). Torrance Test of Creative Thinking. In D. J. Keyser

& R. C. Sweetland (Eds.), *Test critiques* (Vol. VII, pp. 619–622). Kansas City, MO: Test Corporation of America.

Taylor, C. W. (1988). Various approaches to and definitions of creativity. In R. J. Sternberg (Ed.), *The nature of creativity* (pp. 99–121). New York: Cambridge University Press.

Taylor, C. W., & Ellison, R. L. (1966). *Manual for alpha biographical inventory.* Salt Late City, UT: Institute for Behavioral Research in Creativity.

Taylor, C. W., & Ellison, R. L. (1967). Biographical predictors of scientific performance. *Science, 155,* 1075–1080.

Taylor, C. W., & Holland, J. (1964). Predictors of creative performance. In C. W. Taylor (Ed.), *Creativity: Progress and potential* (pp. 15–48). New York: McGraw-Hill.

Thorndike, R. L. (1972). Review of Torrance Tests of Creativity Thinking. In O. K. Buros (Ed.), *The seventh mental measurements yearbook* (pp. 838–839). Highland Park, NJ: Gryphon Press.

Thurstone, L. L. (1938). *Primary mental abilities.* Chicago: University of Chicago Press.

Tierney, P., & Farmer, S. M. (2002). Creative self-efficacy: Its potential antecedents and relationship to creative performance. *Academy of Management Journal, 45*: 1137–1148.

Torrance, E. P. (1962). *Guiding creative talent.* Englewood Cliffs, NJ: Prentice-Hall.

Torrance, E. P. (1965). *Rewarding creative behavior.* Englewood Cliffs, NJ: Prentice-Hall.

Torrance, E. P. (1966). *The Torrance Tests of Creative Thinking—Norms— Technical Manual Research Edition—Verbal Tests, Forms A and B—Figural Tests, Forms A and B.* Princeton NJ: Personnel Press.

Torrance, E. P. (1967). *Understanding the fourth grade slump in creative thinking.* Washington, DC: U. S. Office of Education. (ERIC Document Reproduction Service No. ED 018 273)

Torrance, E. P. (1968). A longitudinal examination of the fourth grade slump in creativity. *Gifted Child Quarterly, 12,* 195–199.

Torrance, E. P. (1969). Prediction of adult creative achievement among high school seniors. *Gifted Child Quarterly, 13,* 223–229.

Torrance, E. P. (1970). *Encouraging creativity in the classroom.* Dubuque, IA: William C. Brown Company Publishers.

Torrance, E. P. (1971). Stimulation, enjoyment, and originality in dyadic creativity. *Journal of Educational Psychology, 62,* 45–48.

Torrance, E. P. (1972a). Can we teach children to think creatively? *Journal of Creative Behavior, 6,* 114–143.

Torrance, E. P. (1972b). *Torrance Tests of Creative Thinking: Directions manual and scoring guide. Figural test booklet A* (Rev. ed.). Bensenville, IL: Scholastic Testing Service.

Torrance, E. P. (1974a). *Torrance Tests of Creative Thinking—Directions manual and scoring guide. Verbal test booklet A.* Bensenville, IL: Scholastic Testing Service.

Torrance, E. P. (1974b). *Torrance Tests of Creative Thinking—Norms— technical manual.* Bensenville, IL: Scholastic Testing Service.

Torrance, E. P. (1975). *Preliminary manual: Ideal Child Checklist.* Athens, GA: Georgia Studies of Creative Behavior.

Torrance, E. P. (1976). Creativity testing in education. *The Creative Child and Adult Quarterly, 1,* 136–148.

Torrance, E. P. (1979). Unique needs of the creative child and adult. In A. H. Passow (Ed.), *The gifted and talented: Their education and development. 78th NSSE Yearbook* (pp. 352–371). Chicago: The National Society for the Study of Education.

Torrance, E. P. (1981a). Empirical validation of criterion-referenced indicators of creative ability through a longitudinal study. *Creative Child and Adult Quarterly, 6,* 136–140.

Torrance, E. P. (1981b). Predicting the creativity of elementary school children (1958–1980)—and the teacher who "made a difference." *Gifted Child Quarterly, 25,* 55–62.

Torrance, E. P. (1981c). *Thinking creatively in action and movement.* Bensonville, IL: Scholastic Testing Service.

Torrance, E. P. (1984). Sounds and images productions of elementary school pupils as predictors of the creative achievements of young adults. *Creative Child and Adult Quarterly, 7,* 8–14.

Torrance, E. P. (1988). The nature of creativity as manifest in its testing. In R. J. Sternberg (Ed.), *The nature of creativity* (pp. 43–75). New York: Cambridge University Press.

Torrance, E. P. (1990). *The Torrance Tests of Creative Thinking—Norms— Technical Manual—Figural (Streamlined) Forms A & B.* Bensenville, IL: Scholastic Testing Service.

Torrance, E. P. (2000). Preschool creativity. *The psychoeducational assessment of preschool children* (3rd ed.). Bracken, B. A. (Ed.), 349–363. Needham Heights, MA: Allyn & Bacon.

Torrance, E. P. (2008). The Torrance Tests of Creative Thinking Norms- Technical Manual Figural (Streamlined) Forms A & B. Bensenville, IL: Scholastic Testing Service.

Torrance, E. P., & Ball, O. E. (1984). *Torrance Tests of Creative Thinking: Streamlined administration and scoring manual* (Rev. ed.). Bensonville, IL: Scholastic Testing Service.

Torrance, E. P., & Gupta, R. K. (1964). *Programmed experiences in creative thinking. Final report on Title VII Project to the U.S. Office of Education.* Minneapolis, MN: Bureau of Educational Research, University of Minnesota.

Torrance, E. P., Khatena, J., & Cunnington, B. F. (1973). *Thinking creatively with sounds and words.* Bensonville, IL: Scholastic Testing Service.

Torrance, E. P., & Myers, R. E. (1971). *Creative learning and teaching.* New York: Dodd, Mead & Company.

Torrance, E. P., & Presbury, J. (1984). The criteria of success used in 242 recent experimental studies of creativity. *Creative Child & Adult Quarterly, 9,* 238–243.

Torrance, E. P., & Safter, H. T. (1989). The long range predictive validity of the Just Suppose Test. *Journal of Creative Behavior, 23,* 219–223.

Torrance, E. P. & Sisk, D. (1997). *Gifted and talented children in the regular classroom.* Buffalo, NY: Creative Education Foundation Press.

Torrance, E. P., Tan, C. A., & Allman, T. (1970). Verbal originality and teacher behavior: A predictive validity study. *The Journal of Teacher Education, 21,* 335–341.

Torrance, E. P., & Wu, T. H. (1981). A comparative longitudinal study of the adult creative achievement of elementary school children identified as highly intelligent and as highly creative. *Creative Child and Adult Quarterly, 6,* 71–76.

Treffinger, D. J. (1985). *Review of the Torrance Tests of Creative Thinking.* In J. V. Mitchell, Jr. (Ed.), *The ninth mental measurements yearbook* (pp. 1632–1634). Lincoln, NE: University of Nebraska.

Treffinger, D. J. (1989). *Student invention evaluation kit: Field test edition.* Sarasota, FL: Center for Creative Learning.

Vail, P. L. (1990). Gifts, talents, and the dyslexias: Wellsprings, springboards, and finding Foley's rocks. *Annals of Dyslexia, 40,* 3–17.

Walker, A. M., Koestner, R., & Hum, A. (1995). Personality correlates of depressive style in autobiographies of creative achievers. *Journal of Creative Behavior, 29,* 75–94.

Wallach, M. A. (1976, January-February). Tests tell us little about talent. *American Scientist,* 57–63.

Wallach, M. A., & Kogan, N. (1965). *Modes of thinking in young children: A study of the creativity-intelligence distinction.* New York: Holt, Rinehart and Winston.

Wallach, M. A., & Wing, C. W., Jr. (1969). *The talented student: A validation of the creativity-intelligence distinction.* New York: Holt, Rinehart and Winston.

Walpole, M.B., Burton, N.W., Kanyi, K., & Jackenthal, A. (2001). *Selecting successful graduate students: In-depth interviews with GRE users.* (GRE Board Research Rep. No. 99–11R, ETS Research Rep. 02–8) Princeton, NJ: Educational Testing Service.

Wechsler, D. (2003). *Manual for the Wechsler Intelligence Scale for Children* (3rd ed.). San Antonio, TX: Psychological Corporation.

Wechsler, S. (2006). Validity of the Torrance Tests of Creative Thinking to the Brazilian culture. *Creativity Research Journal, 18,* 15–25.

Weisberg, R. W. (1993). *Creativity: Beyond the myth of genius.* New York: W. H. Freeman and Company.

Weisberg, R. W. (2006). *Creativity: Understanding Innovation in Problem Solving, Science, Invention, and the Arts.* New York: Wiley.

Westberg, K. L. (1991). The effects of instruction in the inventing process on students' development of inventions. *Dissertation Abstracts International,* 51. (University Microfilms No. 9107625)

Westby, E. L., & Dawson, V. L. (1995). Creativity: Asset or burden in the classroom? *Creativity Research Journal, 8*(1), 1–10.

Williams, F. (1980). *Creativity Assessment Packet.* Buffalo, NY: DOK Publishers.

Wolfradt, U., & Pretz, J. E. (2001). Individual differences in creativity: Personality, story writing, and hobbies. *European Journal of Personality, 15,* 297–310.

Woodcock, R. W., McGrew, K. S., & Mather, N. (2001). *Woodcock-Johnson III Tests of Cognitive Abilities.* Itasca, IL: Riverside.

Woodrum, D. T., & Savage, L. B. (1994). Children who are learning disabled/gifted: Where do they belong? *Educational Research, 36,* 83–89.

Wu, C. H., Cheng, Y., Ip, H. M., & McBride-Chang, C. (2005). Age differences in creativity: Task structure and knowledge base. *Creativity Research Journal, 17,* 321–326.

Yamada, H., & Tam, A. Y.-W. (1996). Prediction study of adult creative achievement: Torrance's longitudinal study of creativity revisited. *Journal of Creative Behavior, 30,* 144–149.

Yamamoto, K. (1964a). Threshold of intelligence in academic achievement of highly creative students. *Journal of Experimental Education, 32,* 401–405.

Yamamoto, K. (1964b). A further analysis of the role of creative thinking in high-school achievement. *Journal of Psychology, 58,* 277–283.

Yoon, S. N. (2006). Comparing the intelligence and creativity scores of Asian American gifted students with Caucasian gifted students. Unpublished doctoral dissertation, Purdue University.

Young, J. W. (1998). Test review of Gifted Education Scale (2nd ed.). In B. S. Plake & J. C. Impara (Eds.), *The fourteenth mental measurements year-*

book [Electronic version]. Retrieved January 9, 2008, from the Buros Institute's *Test Reviews Online* website: http://www.unl.edu/buros

Zhiyan, T., & Singer, J. L. (1996). Daydreaming styles, emotionality, and the big five personality dimensions. *Imagination, Cognition, and Personality, 16,* 399–414.

Ziv, A. (1980). Humor and creativity. *Creative Child and Adult Quarterly, 5,* 159–170.

Annotated Bibliography

Amabile, T. M. (1996). *Creativity in context: Update to the Social Psychology of Creativity.* Boulder, CO: Westview.

This revision of Amabile's (1982) work is a terrific primer about the Consensual Assessment Technique and the relationship of creativity and motivation. Her original book is also worth seeking out.

Baer, J.(1993). *Creativity and divergent thinking: A task-specific approach.* Hillsdale, NJ: Lawrence Erlbaum.

This book examines the domain generality-specificity issue, and also provides many examples of how the Consensual Assessment Technique has been used in research.

Finke, Ronald A., Ward, Thomas B., & Smith, Steven M. (1996). *Creative cognition: Theory, research, and applications* (New Ed.). Boston: The MIT Press.

Finke, Ward, and Smith propose the Geneplore model of creative cognition, which examines both generation and exploration in the world of ideas.

Guilford, J. P. (1967). *The nature of human intelligence.* New York: McGraw-Hill.

Although out of print, this classic work is still available in most libraries.

Kaufman, J. C., & Baer, J. (Eds). (2005). *Creativity across domains: Faces of the muse.* Mahwah, NJ: Lawrence Erlbaum

This collection of essays explores what it means to be creative across many different domains, such as music, writing poetry, science, and teaching.

Kaufman, J. C., & Sternberg, R. J. (Eds). (2006). *The international handbook of creativity*. Cambridge: Cambridge University Press.

This edited volume is a collection of essays from international scholars in 15 different countries. Much of the research and theories discussed in this volume have never been published before in English.

Piirto, J. A. (2004). *Understanding creativity*. Scottsdale, AZ: Great Potential Press.

In this overview of the field, Piirto discusses her model of the Seven I's—Inspiration, Imagery, Imagination, Intuition, Insight, Incubation, and Improvisation.

Runco, M. A. (2007). *Creativity: Theories and themes: Research, development, and practice*. San Diego, CA: Academic Press.

This comprehensive textbook about creativity covers the field from a broad perspective.

Sawyer, R. K. (2006). *Explaining creativity: The science of human innovation*. Oxford, UK: Oxford University Press.

This book takes a sociocultural focus, arguing that creativity can be understood only in the social and cultural contexts in which it occurs. According to Sawyer, an idea that is creative in one sociocultural milieu might not be in another.

Simonton, D. K. (2004). *Creativity in science: Chance, logic, genius, and zeitgeist*. Cambridge: Cambridge University Press.

Simonton tackles the question of eminent creativity in science, analyzing the many factors that comprise scientific genius.

Sternberg, R. J. (Ed.) (1988). *The nature of creativity*. Cambridge: Cambridge University Press.

Although this book is 20 years old, it continues to be a collection of essays by some of the top names in the field.

Sternberg, R. J. (Ed.) (1999). *Handbook of creativity*. Cambridge: Cambridge University Press.

This edited volume includes essays by many of the top researchers on creativity. Several chapters focus on the assessment of creativity (include an essay by Renzulli and Plucker on psychometric approaches).

Sternberg, R. J. (2003). *WICS: Wisdom, intelligence, and creativity, synthesized.* Cambridge: Cambridge University Press.

Sternberg proposes the WICS theory in this book, which integrates creativity into a model that also highlights intelligence and wisdom.

Sternberg, Robert J., Grigorenko, Elena L., & Singer, Jerome L. (2004). *Creativity: From potential to realization.* Washington, DC: American Psychological Association.

Like Kaufman and Baer's (2004) edited volume, this book also includes essays about the domain-specific or domain-general nature of creativity.

Weisberg, Robert W. (2006). *Creativity: Understanding innovation in problem solving, science, invention, and the arts.* New York: Wiley.

Weisberg argues that the thinking processes used by the average person when being creative are the same as those used by geniuses. Even if the final product may not be remembered for generations, we are all capable of productive and creative thought.

Index

About the Authors

James C. Kaufman, PhD, is an Associate Professor at California State University at San Bernardino, where he is also the director of the Learning Research Institute. He received his PhD from Yale University in Cognitive Psychology. Dr. Kaufman's research focuses on the nurturance, structure, and assessment of creativity, as well as the role of creativity and other non-cognitive assessments in student success. Kaufman is the author or editor of 13 books either published or in press. These books include *The Creativity Conundrum* (with Robert Sternberg and Jean Pretz), *Creativity Across Domains: Faces of the Muse* (with John Baer, Lawrence Erlbaum, 2004), *The International Handbook of Creativity* (with Robert Sternberg; Cambridge, 2006), *Creativity and Reason in Cognitive Development* (with John Baer; Cambridge, 2006), and *Applied Intelligence* (with Robert Sternberg and Elena Grigorenko; Cambridge, 2008). His research has been featured on CNN, NPR, BBC, and in *The New York Times*.

Kaufman is a founding co-editor of the official journal for APA's Division 10, *Psychology, Aesthetics, and the Arts*. He is also the Associate Editor of *Journal of Creativity Behavior* and is the Series Editor of the "Psych 101" series from Springer Publishing. He received the 2003 Daniel E. Berlyne Award from Division 10 of the American Psychological Association for outstanding research by a junior scholar, and has received awards for his professional contributions from CSUSB's Psychology Department and their College of Social and Behavioral Sciences.

Jonathan A. Plucker, PhD, is professor of Educational Psychology and Cognitive Science at Indiana University, where he directs the Center for Evaluation and Education Policy. He is also the current President of the Society for the Psychology of Aesthetics, Creativity, and the Arts, which is Division 10 of the American Psychological Association. Professor Plucker's research interests include creativity and intelligence, education policy, and giftedness and talent development, and he has written over 100 publications on these topics. He is especially interested in nontraditional approaches to public education and P-16 education issues, including the incorporation of creativity education into the education systems of developing countries. His most recent book is *Critical Issues and Practices in Gifted Education,* edited with Carolyn Callahan.

He has received numerous awards for his work, including the E. Paul Torrance Award from the National Association for Gifted Children, the Robert C. Berlyne Award from APA Division 10, and several teaching and instructional development awards. Before arriving at IU in 1997, Professor Plucker taught elementary and high school science, received his doctorate in Educational Psychology from the University of Virginia, and taught at the University of Maine. He enjoys spending time with his family and traveling to unique destinations.

Dr. John Baer is a Professor of Educational Psychology at Rider University. He earned his BA from Yale University and his PhD in Cognitive and Developmental Psychology from Rutgers University.

Dr. Baer's research on the development of creativity and his teaching have both won national awards, including the American Psychological Association's Berlyne Prize. His books include *Creativity and Divergent Thinking: A Task-Specific Approach; Creative Teachers, Creative Students; Creativity Across Domains: Faces of the Muse; Reason and Creativity in Development;* and *Are We Free: Psychology and Free Will.* He serves on the editorial board of four educational and cognitive psychology journals.

Dr. Baer has taught at all levels from elementary through graduate school; served as a supervisor of gifted/talented programs for a large public school system; directed a statewide summer program for creatively gifted students; served as a state Director of the "Odyssey of the Mind" Creative Problem-Solving Competition (MD); and served as a consultant to many groups including the Union of Concerned Scientists, the National Education Association, and many local school systems in the areas of promoting creative thinking and writing. His research has been supported by grants from the National Science Foundation, the Educational Testing Service, the National Center for Educational Statistics, and the Carnegie Foundation.